The Church Responds

Joan Thatcher

The Church Responds

Judson Press, Valley Forge

To my father and mother

CONTENTS

Introduction

1

BEING THE CHURCH
IN AN UP-TIGHT WORLD

Glide Memorial United Methodist Church keeps its windows open to the world. When members of the congregation arrive at the front door of this church in downtown San Francisco, they find smiling young people holding clipboards with sign-up sheets for Task Forces or community petitions. Inside the sanctuary, as the clang of cable cars reminds them of the world outside, worshipers discover that ferment is a sign of life.

Accenting a ministry of response to community needs, Glide sees itself as a bridge between the church members and the non-church public. The highly flexible structure of the church depends jointly upon the Sunday worship services and the Glide Community Meetings which follow the worship service on alternate Sundays. In these meetings Task Forces are suggested to help solve community problems. Needs range from teenage runaways to homosexuals, from urban renewal to senior citizens with welfare tangles, from black youngsters who need tutoring to artists and folk musicians who want to share their abilities with an understanding audience.

The new title used for the preaching minister indicates Glide's belief that worship and action cannot be separated in the Christian community. In this United Methodist congregation, A. Cecil Williams is known as the "minister of involvement and celebration." Leaving no doubt about why Glide church is involved, he declares firmly: "The inability to be human is to stand on the sidelines, watching the needs of the world go by and doing nothing. To humanize life is to refuse to make people into things. We keep people at a distance with words, billy clubs, or guns. The Christian man is the responsible man among men, who works to be human, who lives for others."

NEW WINESKINS OR NEW WINE

When a European theologian left the United States after a lecture trip, he said: "I have heard a great deal of talk about new shapes of American church life. Perhaps the real question is whether what is needed is new wineskins or new wine!" Scores of church leaders are sure that concerns about new forms of ministry must not overpower the concern to have the essence of the gospel shine through clearly, whatever shape the new wineskins may take.

The basic rediscovery of the church renewal movement seems to be that worship and service belong together in the Christian life. As the Quakers and Mennonites have always known, a delicate balance is needed between reflection and involvement, prayer and protest marches. This combination is equally valid for individuals and for congregations.

At the Last Supper Jesus called his followers to practice two things "in remembrance of me." The first was symbolized by the bread and wine of the communion meal. The second was dramatized by the towel and basin as Jesus washed the travel-stained feet of his disciples. The commandments to love both God and neighbor have not changed in two thousand years, despite radical differences in the ways these twin commitments are carried out.

Modern churchmen are discovering that a Christian's basic commitment is not to a branch of the institutional church located at Seventh and Pine but to the One who calls each of his followers to be "a man for others." Once he has made a commitment to love God and neighbor, the Christian is sustained by worship, fellowship, and service in the community of faith.

As these discoveries and their consequences create ferment in the church, Christians should keep an open mind toward new ideas and remember that ferment is a sign of life. For local congregations, the option is literally "change or die."

Although it still sounds an uncertain trumpet, the contemporary church is coming to understand that it exists for the world, not for itself. It is called of God to be a servant in the world—through presence, dialogue, and mission. The local church cannot do everything, but it can do something. The rigid idea that all programming belongs inside church walls is crumbling as members find that the outward journey demands their active participation in the life of the world.

Many churches still suffer from the "ingrown toenail syndrome." Listening to some members, one might conclude that new carpeting for the center aisle, the tantrums of the contralto, or planning the women's meeting for May had an importance equivalent to man's first steps on the moon.

From Woonsocket to Waikiki men and women are discovering that they *can* change the church, that genuine and lasting renewal is possible for persons, programs, and organizational structures. Such change is neither easy nor automatic, but it is possible.

If the smaller group that makes up the inner core of a church becomes firmly committed to renewal in all its dimensions, the members of such a group will invest in both worship and service all the time and energy they possess. To express their concern for the larger group of fringe members and those who label themselves outsiders, this core group may explore the possibilities of vital communication in some kind of neutral setting. The stained-glass atmosphere of the sanctuary may be temporarily forsaken for the informality of a living room or the accessibility of a conference room at a bank; the silver chalice may be exchanged for a coffee cup.

The world is already far along the road to unbelief. The gap between the church and the world has grown so wide that it defies the customary bridges. Both "new wine" and "new wineskins" are needed. For those on the inside, "new wine" is often found in depth Bible study, in small encounter groups, and in vital, contemporary worship services. For those on the outside, "new wineskins" which develop into new shapes of ministry within and beyond the local church may become bridges for two-way traffic between church and world.

The renewal-seeking church need not give up its Sunday morning service or its chaplaincy-to-families ministry. Instead, it should make the sacrifices required to *add* some form of service that will relate the church in a valid way to the life of the world.

After an intensive study of nine Presbyterian churches, Grace Ann Goodman wrote in *Rocking the Ark: "These two points— revitalized members and community-serving programs—seem to add up to a good working definition of 'renewal.' "* She concluded: "It takes only a remnant of God's people to start rocking the ark."[1]

Most outsiders ignore the church because they feel its activities are trivial or because they believe the church has no interest in their concerns or in them as persons, except perhaps to sign them up on the membership rolls. As soon as Christians drag traditional God-talk into the conversation, the outsiders tune out.

A difficult but effective way to overcome this barrier is to establish listening ministries. These take many forms, including coffee houses, tutoring, counseling services, and film discussion groups within the local church. Community action projects, industrial missions, apartment house and shopping center ministries, and night pastors—all ecumenical in approach—are usually financed and directed by a group of local churches.

Churches used to act as though evangelism and service were totally separate functions. Now, with a new theological understanding of sanctification, these roles have become blended. Christian morality is no longer measured by what a man does not do—drink, smoke, swear, gamble—but by the positive Christian qualities of love and justice, openness and authenticity. This morality is based on the premise that God accepts all men just as they are.

When the church labors incognito in one of these ministries, it should not do so with a hidden agenda. Someone has said, "Jesus did not feed the five thousand because they were good, but because they were hungry." The Gospels include no record that he insisted that the people he helped should turn up for church on Sunday morning, or join the choir, or send their children to church school. The multitude needed his help, and he gave it—as simply as that.

Every church must choose the role of guest or servant in the city. Only a few landmark churches can survive as guests. The others must realize that usefulness is the rent they pay for room on earth. They will recognize that sacrificial stewardship is one of the ways a congregation can test whether it is experiencing renewal. If enough members have been persuaded that something really needs doing and that it is up to their church to do it, they will reorganize their priorities to give the time needed and change their giving habits to pay the bills.

Patience is another prerequisite for church renewal. Careful surveys of needs and preparation for action may easily take two years or longer. Bad Boll Academy, Sheffield Industrial Mission, and other European and American ventures have insisted that five years is the barest minimum in which a new project can be firmly launched. The more radical the idea, the more time people take to become convinced it is worth trying. Like new shoes, changes in church organization, liturgy, or value scales may pinch highly sensitive spots.

In expressing his philosophy about change and conflict, one minister said:

> You have to move the congregation along with you. Some leaders think I move too slowly, but I say they're like a landing party that doesn't bother to ready the longboats. Instead, they recklessly break up the mother ship and float ashore on the planks. Then when the natives attack, there's nobody in reserve. You have to have the congregation somewhere nearby, floating off-shore so to speak, but in shouting range. You get the members to come along by building trust, by always being absolutely honest and developing the reputation of absolute integrity and not trying to put something over on them. This takes a lot of talking with the key leaders, so they come to trust you as a person even if they don't agree with everything you want to do.[3]

AREAS OF FERMENT

There are a number of ways in which the bubbling new wine is threatening the old wineskins of the organized church.

Changing Roles of Clergy and Laymen. One of the most drastic shifts in church patterns has been the changing role of the clergy. Leaders are realizing that specialization is as necessary for the church as it is for the field of medicine. Just as a pediatrician is not expected to do a heart transplant, so the church should not expect all of its ministers to be equally expert in every specialized area of ministry.

Many creative churches are broadening the base of their programming by supporting a ministry outside the parish structure or by adding or retraining staff to develop new outreaches within the church walls.

Also, many ministers no longer want to be seen as *the* authority figure in the local church. Granting considerable uncertainty of method, nearly all ministers striving for church renewal are attempting to encourage heavy lay involvement in all phases of church life, from planning buildings and budgets to calling in homes and preaching dialogue sermons.

Most younger clergymen agree that their role is not that of a "holy man" who performs the church's ministry, but that of a theologically trained catalyst or change-agent who assists laymen in seeking out their own forms of Christian service. As one Philadelphia minister said, "I can go out and picket until the cows come home, but that won't mean a whole lot. My real job is to make people aware of their own responsibilities to help change the structures of society by what they do from nine to five."

Since the laity are the agents of reconciliation in the world, they need serious study and training programs to equip them for mission and specific action projects to enable them to serve others. Along with the basics of the Christian faith, the needs of persons and the issues which confront them should determine the content of the church program. Decisions about programs ought to be based on careful surveys of needs and preferences. Program planning should be stripped to essentials and organizational structures and fund raising streamlined, so that time, energy, and money can be concentrated on mission, not on mechanics.

Mortgages and Mission. In congregation after congregation, the first reaction to suggestions for bold new programs of church renewal is: "But we can't possibly afford it!" When pressed about why they can't, church leaders point to the large percentage of the annual budget which must be spent for mortgage payments and interest and for maintaining the church property—everything from heat and light to landscaping and the custodian's salary. The operating cost for Riverside Church or St. Patrick's Cathedral in New York City is estimated to be about $1500 per day, with the costs for smaller church buildings scaled down accordingly.

The biblical drama began in a garden and ended in a city, not in a Gothic sanctuary. Jesus opened his public ministry in his hometown synagogue in Nazareth, and during the final week of his earthly ministry he dramatically evicted the moneychangers from the temple in Jerusalem. In between these events, he preached and counseled where the people were—on the mountainside, at the village well, in the homes of friends. This kind of ministry hardly seems to provide a biblical basis for the cult of church building which has emerged in twentieth-century America.

Until the eighth century, churches had one cathedral per town, with small chapels in outlying sections. Then people apparently decided that a church's prestige was measured by the size and magnificence of its building. A construction boom began in the Middle Ages and is only now beginning to slow down. When many churches face massive mortgage payments which strangle the annual budget, they recognize that they have "overbuilt."

Several types of changes are taking place in church building plans. Among major denominations, the East Harlem Protestant Parish pioneered in 1948 with storefront locations. These appear more accessible to people who are unfamiliar with Gothic arches, and most of the budget is kept free for staff and programming for mission. Some experimental congregations have decided they simply don't intend to construct a building. They meet in homes, stores, or theaters.

Occasionally pairs of congregations share physical facilities on a staggered time basis. Instead of the usual Christian education wing, other churches have developed new multipurpose facilities used throughout the week for community service programs.

When Fulton J. Sheen was bishop of the Roman Catholic diocese of Rochester, he issued stern orders that all church building plans be examined with one eye on the plight of the poor. He also required that an amount equal to 3 percent of every parish construction project be contributed to humanitarian programs. Unfinished cathedrals in Washington and San Francisco have been picketed by those who protest what they term an ostentatious display of churchly wealth while men are starving.

Time magazine reports: "Presbyterian Theologian Robert Mc-Afee Brown . . . suggests that the church should be prepared to quarter itself 'in campaign tents rather than cathedrals. That would reflect the mobility of the modern church and allow it to go where the people are.' " [3]

Ecumenical Ministries. A third area of change in the church today is taking place along ecumenical lines. Since Pope John XXIII unleashed the spirit of *aggiornamento,* Protestants have been hurrying to catch up. Some of the earliest ecumenical enthusiasm was channeled into the civil rights movement and peace protests. Often it was the ministers and priests who had met at Selma, Washington, or Atlanta who suggested working together in their home communities.

Nearly all of the new unstructured or "listening" ministries have ecumenical sponsorship. Grass-roots approaches to community problems by groups of churches are gathering momentum. Several Protestant seminaries have appointed Catholic faculty members or joined federations where faculty and library resources are pooled on an interfaith basis.

The Underground Church. The early church began in the first century with small groups meeting secretly in homes, sharing each other's concerns, and partaking together of the bread and wine in remembrance of their Lord. Now the underground church is starting the process all over again.

Catholic theologian Michael Novak has estimated that many thousands of Americans are members of the two thousand to three thousand underground church groups across the nation.[4] Most members of these groups are Catholics, with some Protestants joining in. Often they regard the underground church as the only acceptable bridge between an established church (dominated by the hierarchy and tradition) and the futile attempt to be a Christian apart from any organized group.

Many priests ordained within the last ten years are willing to celebrate the illegal masses, although the elements consecrated may be as unusual as coffee and doughnuts. English is used rather than Latin, and a guitar or piano is the typical musical accompaniment. Most underground groups avoid direct competition with the parish church, but they open the way for church members to experience a smaller, more intense community.

Michael Novak concludes:

> The underground church . . . offers a way of celebrating death and life, community and loneliness, joy and sadness—a way that is at once fresh and spontaneous and yet tied to traditions as old as western man. . . . It teaches those who are too cultic-minded that a man who offers bread to God when other men starve for lack of bread has not understood the gospel of Jesus Christ.[5]

THE CHURCH IN FERMENT

Is the church alive? Is the renewal of the church really possible? After eighteen months of research, my answer is firmly "Yes!"

A key question asked by many young ministers is: "How can Christianity be possible if life in the church is impossible?" They answer the probing question by seeking to mold a church that is a revitalized center capable of dealing calmly with the crucial issues confronting church and nation. They try to wed personal concern with the public good, justice with love, and God's law with man's.

How much renewal is possible in a specific church seems to depend mainly on the courage and organizational skills of the minister and whether the congregation has the insight and flexibility to adopt a mandate for change. Other factors include the attitude of the community, the caliber of denominational leadership, and the point on the spectrum of change where the church begins.[6]

Most of the traditional churches (perhaps half of the total) concentrate on Sunday programming, midweek services, a women's society, and a Boy Scout troop. Renewal efforts in these churches have a long way to go, since change of any kind is apt to be resisted by conservative members of such congregations.

Approximately one-third of the churches have progressed to all-week programming which is designed to meet genuine needs of contemporary Christians. These churches range in size from two hundred to over one thousand members and often have more than one minister. There is much more hope for renewal in these situations, although it must be proposed and carried out with skill and understanding.

Dozens of young ministers today are serving churches that have discovered what it means to be both the gathered congregation within the church and the dispersed congregation in the community where they act as leaven in the world. Eager to participate in the renewal of the church, such ministers number under 10 percent of the total number of ministers, and they serve churches ranging in size from less than one hundred members to more than three thousand. The core members are willing to accept the posture of servanthood—through presence, dialogue, and mission. Where human need exists, these members seek to find solutions. They want their seven-day-a-week lives to say to the world: "The Word has become flesh and dwells among us."

Clearly, the church *is* unfinished, and change is the order of the day for congregations and clergy alike. One result of this ferment and flexibility is that this book is also unfinished. It reports situations as they were observed between June, 1968, and September, 1969, but many program aspects may have changed between then and now.

As these chapters illustrate, scores of ministers have experienced the freedom to reshape their congregations and their ministries so that they can share in the covenant community at the points where their particular capabilities can do the most to meet deep human needs and hungry spirits. Their goal is to help their congregations become the servant church Christ calls them to be.

In creating the ferment that is a sign of life in the church, renewal-minded congregations seek to echo Reinhold Niebuhr's famous prayer:

> God grant me the serenity to accept
> the things I cannot change,
> the courage to change
> the things I can,
> And the wisdom to know the difference.[7]

NOTES

[1] Grace Ann Goodman, *Rocking the Ark* (New York: Board of National Missions, United Presbyterian Church in the U.S.A., 1968), pp. 211, 214.

[2] *Ibid.*, p. 201.

[3] *Time,* January 12, 1968, p. 49.

[4] Michael Novak, "The Underground Church," *Saturday Evening Post,* December 28, 1968—January 11, 1969, pp. 26ff.

[5] *Ibid.*

[6] See Chapter 16 on "Change and Renewal" by Lawrence H. Janssen in this volume for more extended discussion of these factors.

[7] *United Church Herald,* December, 1969.

The Reality-Shaped Parish

2

GLIDE MEMORIAL UNITED METHODIST CHURCH IN SAN FRANCISCO

In the usually critical opinion of *Time* magazine, Glide Memorial United Methodist Church in San Francisco is "probably the nation's most successful and adventurous mission church." [1] The creativity evident in its worship services may also qualify it as the nation's most turned-on church. At least, as San Francisco columnist Herb Caen reports, it is the only church in town that people fight to get into! [2] Every pew is packed, and the ushers have to set up folding chairs.

A major reason for its freedom is the support which the church receives through the Glide Foundation. Sharing an income of $350,000 a year, church and foundation leaders have worked to establish an atmosphere of openness where pioneering is the expected pattern of behavior. Their freedom is not restricted by the need to ask frequently, "Will the people who pay the bills go along with this?" Since the basic budget is assured, the question becomes instead: "What needs to be done, and do we have the courage to do it?"

INVOLVEMENT AND CELEBRATION

A clear note of joy sounds forth in the worship services at Glide, combined with a well-defined concern for the needs of persons and the community at large. Since Cecil Williams became the preaching minister in 1966, there has been a movement toward "black worship," with its freer forms and greater congregational participation. His position is somewhat unique: He is a Texas-born Negro and most of the church members are white. Being on the frontier is not new for him, however. He was one of the first five blacks to be enrolled at Southern Methodist University.

21

Aided by the Events Task Force, Mr. Williams plans many special musical and dramatic services which help to proclaim the Good News in a contemporary setting. Glide's use of jazz quartets, spirituals, and folk music is a deliberate part of the movement of the blacks for dignity, manhood, and a wider recognition of black culture.

Since July, 1969, Sunday morning services have been led by Cecil Williams and the Meridian West or other jazz folk groups. The predominantly white congregation is a mixture of Glide members, adult visitors who obviously belong to the "straight" world, and a goodly number of hippies and other young adults who normally would never go to church anywhere.

The liturgy and the sermons include quotations from Langston Hughes, Malcolm Boyd, Bob Dylan, Simon and Garfunkel, Dietrich Bonhoeffer, and Martin Luther King, Jr. The selections are contemporary in content and solidly rooted in biblical and theological traditions. They are set in a framework of joyous music and an atmosphere that invites response instead of encouraging the sedateness expected in traditional churches.

After an opening hymn, the congregation sings spirituals and folk songs with a lively beat and invariably end up in a hand-clapping rhythm. The worshipers also applaud the prelude, the anthems, and the sermon! Because of the responsive atmosphere, such behavior does not seem out of place.

The pulpit and choir seats were removed from the platform to make room for the grand piano, drums, string bass, and flute. The three ministers process in their black robes and sit in the front pew. Cecil Williams uses a lapel microphone when he speaks from the center, and his associates speak from a side lectern.

In one sermon Mr. Williams said, "Those who are not embracing are not feeling. There's something wrong somewhere, baby!" He concluded: "Agape is important as we try to love the unloved. Eros is also important as we love the lovely. You can't have one without the other."

Response to this turned-on atmosphere is indicated in several ways. Every seat is filled twenty minutes before the service begins, and lines form out on the sidewalk. When the regular offering plates began to overflow with dollar bills, Glide switched to wicker baskets. On a single Sunday in September, 1969, twelve persons joined the church at once.

On one Christmas Eve the street in front of the church was blocked off, and a jazz combo provided music for dancing in the streets. Then everyone was invited into the sanctuary for a concert by Meridian West. During the service, the flutist played "Joy to the World" and led the congregation in a march around the sanctuary. Everyone received a gift of fruit, and for some in the inner city this was the only joyful experience of Christmas.

Cecil Williams has also been strongly identified with the black protest movement, working in the ghetto areas and trying to "cool it" when feelings get out of hand. On the Sunday after the Newark riots, he preached vigorously on "Race, Riots, and Reconciliation." When one speaker had to cancel his appearance during the 1968 meetings of the Methodist Synod of California, Cecil Williams was instrumental in getting Eldridge Cleaver, then a leader of the Black Panthers in Oakland, to speak to the synod for an hour. Mr. Williams felt that there was more serious analysis than he had ever seen in an annual conference session. According to Mr. Williams, the conclusion reached by Mr. Cleaver was starkly realistic: "There is hope for America if we can eliminate racism."

THE FREEDOM TO ACT

Everyone at Glide has the freedom to act as he feels motivated to, whether or not the other ministers or lay leaders agree. In one instance, a seminary intern concluded his research in the Tenderloin area surrounding the church and felt that this section of the city also needed to be named as a poverty area so that it would receive special help through government programs. The Economic Opportunities Council had already decided on four other areas and planned to split the available funds four ways.

After the intern found support for his position, an interesting polarity developed. Two of the original four areas were largely Negro and had strong black power organizations. Cecil Williams, Glide's senior minister, was one of the spokesmen for the Negro areas, Hunter's Point and the Western Addition. While Mr. Williams represented the black establishment inside City Hall, the intern and other whites from the Tenderloin marched around outside, carrying placards and singing "We Shall Overcome." Ultimately, the Tenderloin was also named as a poverty area.

On another occasion, a young volunteer was named chairman of Glide's commission on membership and evangelism, which is part of the usual structure in a Methodist church. Six months later, without telling anyone in advance what he planned to do, Vic stood in the pulpit and explained his belief that this commission fulfilled only a gate-keeping function by screening new members so that they would fit in with those the church already had. Instead, he proposed that people could be freer if they did not have to act out this role, and he proceeded to dissolve the comission then and there. There were small gasps from two persons in the congregation that morning—the national director of evangelism and the head of the board of missions of the Methodist Church, who happened to be visiting.

Since that morning, the vows of membership differ from those in the Methodist Order of Worship and stress that the basic task of Christians is to respond in love to human needs. According to the self-exiled chairman of the commission on membership, who became a Glide intern, the number of Glide members has risen steadily ever since! Vic is one of those who has discovered that at Glide he could change the church, rather than just having the church change him.

"Penetration" and "involvement" are key words as the Glide Urban Center staff seeks in a professional way to get the facts about a specific problem and then tries to "tell it like it is" and do something to change the situation. Generous financial support from the endowment funds of the Glide Foundation enables the center to concentrate on ministry rather than fund-raising. The staff and resources of the Glide Urban Center extend the church's ministry beyond its walls and seek to bring about change in the city. The first reaction of the uninitiated is apt to be shock when he finds Glide sponsoring a dance for homosexuals, a residence for teenage runaways, or a street-corner ministry to young prostitutes and pill-pushers in the Tenderloin area surrounding the church.

TASK FORCES

Task Forces have been used extensively since 1967, when Glide Church found that this method seemed to turn-on young adults, a highly mobile group who want short-term involvement in significant projects. The Task Forces follow no set time schedules but are set up when a need is discovered and end when the project is completed or has been found to be unfeasible. Keeping up with Task Force activity is virtually a full-time job for Lloyd K. Wake, minister of congregational life, assisted by a student intern. Virtually all Task Forces are related directly to one of the various groups of people living in the area surrounding the church.

This Tenderloin district of thirty thousand residents should not be confused with Skid Row or with the black ghettos. The Tenderloin is not very sinister by day, but at night its bars, eating places, and pool halls entertain more than their share of prostitutes, pimps, junkies, racing fans, black-jacketed motorcyclists, homosexuals, and assorted other persons rarely invited into polite society.[3] The area is regarded as the training ground for new prostitutes and homosexuals and is the center of a pill-pushing traffic in Northern California which has been estimated to gross $500,000 a month.[4]

Most of the three thousand young people in the area are from broken homes and have urgent emotional needs for love and acceptance. Often a high school dropout, a young person in the Tenderloin is alone, alienated, and unable to break through the barriers that separate him from other people. In the teenage subculture, he follows the group values and behavior rules of his peers. Often he takes everything he can from those around him and imagines that others will do the same to him. Unfortunately, one hears Californians express more concern for conserving redwood trees than for conserving these bright minds and creative spirits.

Working almost alone, Glide has established a program of streetworkers who appear in certain designated places on a regular nightly schedule. It opened Hospitality House as a drop-in center and hopes to extend this service to include vocational training. Huckleberry House provides temporary housing, meals, and counseling for runaway teenagers, after they have received their parents' permission to stay there.

The maintenance of an extensive educational program inside the church is not considered by members of Glide Church as their most important ministry. Instead, after some false starts, the Educational Task Force began a tutoring program with four or five volunteers who visited black homes in the Western Addition once a week for a tutoring session on a one-to-one basis. Their enthusiasm was so contagious that within six months Glide had sixty tutors, more than half of them from outside the congregation. After an early June picnic with their pupils in Golden Gate Park, the tutors decided some organized summer activities were needed.

As a group, they pooled funds for a storefront location and hastily staffed a lively summer program in the ghetto—before the ministers even found out the tutors were concerned and wanted to provide summer activities.

The St. Francis Task Force was established in 1967, when San Francisco was expecting a summer invasion of one hundred thousand hippies. To achieve their goal of reminding the city that St. Francis was himself a beggar, Task Force members had the saint's most famous prayer set to music and recorded for disc jockey shows and reprinted on billboards and wallet-size cards. Somewhat carried away by their enthusiasm, they even acquired five thousand gaily colored balloons, which they painted with phrases from the prayer and unleashed on the city!

When the expected hippie invasion didn't materialize, the Task Force shifted its energy to aiding the poor. Their principal effort was the Black People's Free Store. Modeled after the Free Store in nearby Haight-Ashbury, it gathers contributions of food, clothing, and household furniture from merchants, church members, and other interested persons. These items are made available on a 24-hour-a-day basis to black people, with no cash expected or strings attached. They just walk in and help themselves to what they need—a suit, a toaster, a table, a refrigerator, a TV set. The staff has largely dissuaded the handful of persons who take things only to sell them to someone else.

Volunteers at Glide provide manpower for projects of other institutions, such as the night ministry of the San Francisco Council of Churches; or people from Glide take tickets, make posters, or serve coffee at Intersection, a center for religion and the arts sponsored by Glide Urban Center and several denominations. They take part in Citizens Alert, a network of citizens on 24-hour duty to receive telephoned reports of police harassment and brutality. Volunteers also assist staff members in jobs which range from stuffing envelopes to hanging an art exhibit, from joining a picket line to interviewing the police chief!

The minister to older persons directs a Task Force which works on Glide's Thursday program for senior citizens. They visit shut-ins and do trouble-shooting for seniors needing help on welfare benefits and other problems. Demonstrating that they have some power, two busloads of senior citizens went to Sacramento to carry placards and meet with legislators to insist that it was wrong for the State of California to reduce welfare benefits to coincide with an increase made in federal Social Security benefits.

Part of Glide's methodology is to launch needed projects and then turn them over to other agencies or groups. The San Francisco United Methodist Mission now sponsors Baker Place, a Glide-initiated halfway house for persons referred from mental health institutions, for unwed mothers, and for referrals from the California Youth Authority.

The Glide Urban Center conducts an impressive program of communications and research, headed by Donald L. Kuhn. Although the Glide church membership is about three hundred, Glide's mailing list totals about three thousand interested persons. Fifteen hundred in the Bay Area alone receive copies of *Venture,* the church newsletter. In a single week in October, 1967, Glide received major coverage in both *Time* and the *Los Angeles Times WEST* magazines. Outstanding photos by Bob Fitch appear in most Glide-published books and on the covers of Sunday bulletins.

Mr. Kuhn has also organized a network of people who are concerned to see change take place to benefit the city. These people joined together in recommending top candidates to the mayor to fill two vacancies on the city's board of education. Skilled volunteers augment the research program by conducting interviews and analyzing voting patterns and other sociometric data.

Glide Foundation is an approved agency for conscientious objectors and acceptable to many local draft boards as a place where alternate-service requirements may be fulfilled. In 1968 about forty C.O.'s were working as unpaid volunteers in various Glide programs. The building houses the offices of the Northern California Chapter of Clergy and Laymen Concerned about Vietnam, and Glide joins in hosting informational programs on draft resistance and the problems of violence, featuring such leading spokesmen as Dr. Robert McAfee Brown, and Joan Baez and her husband, David Harris.

THE GLIDE FOUNDATION

Nearly a half century ago, a rancher named Glide bought sheep land in Kern County and found oil. His philanthropically inclined widow built the church and foundation offices in his memory and then bequeathed one million dollars to Glide Foundation to endow the program. Now the annual income is about $350,000. For many years this was used to underwrite the program of Glide Methodist Church, then a typical white, family-centered congregation, and to make grants for church extension and schools of evangelism.

Surprisingly enough, the change in outreach was brought about largely by the reaction of the foundation's board of directors to some harsh questions asked by the Internal Revenue Service! When the I.R.S. began questioning why the foundation was not using more of its annual income for programs and grants, the directors decided they had better get busy. In 1963 the board employed Lewis E. Durham, a Los Angeles minister, as head of the foundation. He soon brought in Don Kuhn in communications, Cecil Williams in community involvement, and Ted McIlvenna as minister of young adults.

Obviously, Glide's present style of ministry is not everybody's choice, and the church has received a large measure of criticism for some of its far-out activities. Despite this, it has always had the strong backing of the Methodist bishop, a member of the foundation board (whose offices are in the Glide building), and of community leaders such as Willie Brown, San Francisco's first black representative in the California State Assembly. Mr. Durham says firmly, "The church must say yes to all people because God cares about all people." [5]

Perhaps Glide's ministry can best be summed up in the word "Shalom," the peace that passes understanding. It offers "Shalom not only for black people and white people, but Shalom for the too old and the too young, Shalom for the police and for the prostitute, Shalom for the homosexual and the normally sexed, Shalom for husband and wife, and [most of all] Shalom for the disturbed heart of the city." [6]

NOTES

[1] *Time,* October 20, 1967, p. 88.

[2] Column by Herb Caen, *San Francisco Chronicle,* September 16, 1969, p. 17.

[3] Kenneth Lamott, "Nearer, My Church, to Me," *Los Angeles Times WEST* magazine, October 22, 1967.

[4] Edward Hansen, Mark Forrester, and Fred Bird, *The Tenderloin Ghetto: The Young Reject in Our Society* (San Francisco: Glide Urban Center, n.d.), p. 11

[5] *Time,* October 20, 1967, p. 88.

[6] Lamott, *op. cit.*

3

JUDSON MEMORIAL BAPTIST CHURCH IN MINNEAPOLIS

Judson was a typical midwestern residential congregation until 1964 when a creative young minister, J. Richard Fowler, was called to be its pastor. He has turned the church virtually inside out and upside down and kept the support of nearly everyone in doing so. Although the church is related to the American Baptist Convention, a high percentage of the members come from other denominations. New people join the church almost every month, youth programs are growing as never before, and mission giving has more than doubled in five years.

Monthly parish zone meetings led by the deacons discuss such vital issues as the report of the Kerner Commission, the problems of family life today, and a potentially closer relationship between Judson and a nearby Negro church. The cumbersome machinery of the annual every-member canvass has been eliminated. Instead, the budget needs are explained and pledges are received in one of the zone meetings.

The official boards have been streamlined and now meet on the fourth Sunday during the church school hour. Only the executive council meets once a month for an evening session. This schedule frees the ministers and lay people to use their time creatively in parish zones, in interfaith community action projects, and in planning creative worship experiences.

CREATIVE WORSHIP

Young clergymen today believe meaningful worship must be both creative and contemporary so that worshipers will be led to rethink what their faith is all about rather than merely to repeat the same phrases from one Sunday to the next.

The greatest single change at Judson has come in the Sunday

morning service through the combined efforts of Mr. Fowler and Dr. Rudolph Berryman, minister of music and Christian education. After fifty years with a traditional order of worship, Judson members now often experience a Sunday worship service that includes a dialogue sermon, a play, an oratorio, or contemporary music sung by the Judson Folksingers. Even the time of the service has been moved up an hour to encourage more adults to remain for the adult education program which follows. That decision caused some storm clouds on the horizon, but the clouds disappeared and the people came.

A dialogue sermon on poverty and affluence was given by a young pediatrician who works in a poverty area clinic and the coordinator of federal programs for Minnesota's department of education. Another dialogue sermon on understanding marriage was a conversation between the minister and a seminary professor who teaches courses on Christian faith and human personality. When a nearby Negro congregation returned an exchange visit by 310 Judson members, they heard a dialogue sermon by Mr. Fowler and Miss Lillian Anthony, director of the Mayor's Commission on Human Rights.

The Judson Folksingers were organized in 1967 and are in demand for programs throughout the state. Occasionally they sing at Sunday morning services, although the congregation has requested that the music on communion Sundays be more traditional. The enthusiasm of the two young ministers and their awareness of today's world, coupled with innovations in worship and programming, have meant that participation by young people has grown from a handful to sometimes half the congregation.

The Christmas Eve service one year included a musical combo and an interpretation in modern dance; the next year's service was a more traditional presentation of lessons and carols.

Four Lenten sermons interpreted the meaning of Vivaldi's *Gloria,* which was then sung in its entirety as the Easter morning service, under Dr. Berryman's direction. On Maundy Thursday communion is served around tables in the fellowship hall in a setting similar to the early church. One Palm Sunday morning the Judson Players presented *Casey,* a dramatic meditation on the passion of our Lord. The play probes the problems of racial prejudice, the generation gap, the misuse of sex, and the seeming inability of the church to cope meaningfully with these problems.

ECUMENICAL EXPLORATION

An even more significant break with tradition has been Judson's exploration with other faiths. Interaction with Temple Israel began with music and drama. The Judson Players presented a docu-drama on social issues, and discussion followed. Then groups from both congregations attended performances at the Tyrone Guthrie Theater.

Events with two neighborhood churches, Incarnation Roman Catholic parish and St. John's Lutheran, began even more cautiously. In 1967 the Judson Women's Guild and the parish zones invited the members of Incarnation to see and discuss the award-winning film, *La Strada*. Youth from Judson and Incarnation planned some joint weekend retreats. During two summers, youth from all three churches produced *Brigadoon* and *Oklahoma* with proceeds used for the support of ecumenical ministries in the neighborhood.

A full-scale ecumenical dialogue was held during Lent in 1968. On the three Wednesday evenings preceding Holy Week, the three congregations met together at 7 P.M. for worship. Then fifty persons selected from each church remained at 7:30 for discussions on baptism, the eucharist, and liturgy. Judson members heard Sunday sermons highlighting the Baptist position on each theme. On Palm Sunday evening, the combined choirs and an orchestra from the three churches presented *St. John's Passion* by Handel. That fall Hobart Methodist joined the other three churches for an interfaith service of worship on Thanksgiving Eve.

DEEPENING RELATIONSHIPS

The challenging human concerns which are murmured in the pastor's study any week of the year would astonish anyone who has never done personal counseling. In the time it takes his office door to swing open, the minister must be able to go from sorrow to joy, from a divorce to a marriage.

Now engaged in completing his doctoral studies on counseling and family life, Dick Fowler is highly skilled in the field of counseling. He has led extremely popular retreats for Judson couples on the subject of communication in marriage and inaugurated a series of four Sunday evening discussions on this theme, which culminated in an overnight "communication marathon."

Sensitivity training sessions have also been held for the

young people participating in the annual Judson Youth Caravan. On one caravan trip, after a year of serious study of ethics and value systems, thirteen high school young people took off with Mr. Fowler and another counselor in a rented airport limousine to travel 5,200 miles through the western United States. Using sleeping bags in tents and church basements, they explored first-hand the kinds of ethics and value systems followed in Salt Lake City, Reno, San Francisco's Chinatown and Haight-Ashbury. Along the way they visited the I-Thou coffee house in Haight-Ashbury and a gambling casino, toured the redwood forests, saw Mount Rushmore by flashlight, and camped in the majestic mountains of the Grand Tetons. By living together twenty-four hours a day, they came to know each other as persons and how they really felt about things that matter.

The hippies of Haight-Ashbury seemed to make the greatest impression. In a group dialogue sermon on the young people's first Sunday back, one girl explained to the congregation, "Looking at hippies on the outside turns you off, because their dress is so odd and you're sure they haven't seen a bathtub lately. You're forced to look on the inside to try to understand them. They are genuinely trying to find themselves and the meaning of life."

Recognizing that the best opportunity to deepen the meaning of membership comes at the time people decide to join the church, Judson has radically altered its program of preparing young people for church membership. Previously, classes were held on six Saturday mornings during Lent. Now Dr. Berryman directs a three-year program which constitutes the church school curriculum for the seventh, eighth, and ninth grades.

The program during the first two years stresses developing a sense of community. Realizing that Judson youth come from many different schools, this purpose is fulfilled through weekend retreats, canoe trips, and excursions. Ministers and youth alike have learned that curriculum content can be covered in more depth during a weekend retreat program once a month than during six weeks of Sunday church school with its varying attendance problems. Study during these years uses films as a catalyst for learning with biblical assignments related to the film's message. *No Exit, Raisin in the Sun, David and Lisa,* and *Cry, the Beloved Country* are among the films the youth have seen, paralleling their study of the major personalities of the Bible.

Ninth graders focus their attention on the Bible, beliefs of the church, and Christian ethics. They write several major papers and must take a content examination on each area. The parents study with their teenagers throughout the year, both in all-day sessions held about once a month and in home preparations.

Early in May the deacons share an hour and a half of discussion with the young people, and each ninth grader has an oral review with Mr. Fowler. After this preparation, the young people are asked individually if membership in the church, with its accompanying responsibilities, would be meaningful. Those who affirm this commitment make their confession of faith and are baptized during a Sunday morning service. The others are encouraged to make their commitment at a later date.

This training is followed by two more years of preparation in Christian vocation, self-understanding, ecumenics, and world religions. The preparation culminates in a service of commissioning for the "scattered ministries" of the Christian faith at work in the world.

THE ACID TEST

The crucial test of whether the "priesthood of all believers" really works began at Judson in August, 1969, when Mr. Fowler left for fifteen months in Florida to complete his doctorate in counseling. At this writing it is still in progress.

Preaching during the interim period is done by seven ministers related to the congregation, five lay members, and guest speakers including Dr. Harvey Cox, Dr. Elton Trueblood, author Keith Miller, and Father Godfrey Diekman.

Rather than the usual practice of securing an interim minister, the Judson congregation decided to employ one of its lay leaders, Harold tenBensel, as the church administrator. He also works half time for St. John's Lutheran Church two blocks away. An accountant at General Mills for thirty-five years, Mr. tenBensel and his family have been mainstays at Judson for three decades. He was church school superintendent for fifteen years and also has been a trustee, deacon, scoutmaster, and chairman of the board of Christian education.

A recently retired couple, Mr. and Mrs. Willard Esau, serve as church visitors on a volunteer basis. They, along with Mr. tenBensel, Dr. Berryman, and the board of deacons, call on shut-ins and hospital patients.

As minister of music and Christian education, Dr. Berryman supervise the junior high fellowship and also work with seven advisors for senior highs and young adults. Arrangements for weddings and funerals are made by Mr. tenBensel or Dr. Berryman, and services are conducted by three ordained ministers from the congregation. The counseling program is carried out by Dr. Berryman and by a physician, a seminary professor, and three other trained counselors who are Judson members.

The interim experiment was conceived by Mr. Fowler as a test of the tentmaking ministry idea, which means that each member of the congregation is literally seen as one of the ministers. In an interview he said: "What Rudi Berryman and I would like to do is to work ourselves out of a job by having the members really become the ministers at Judson. We believe they can do it."

Creativity and challenge are usually welcomed by Judson members because they have been prepared to expect change and to accept challenges. Without fanfare and in a spirit of deep understanding, unusual things are done simply because they need doing and it seems logical for Judson to do them.

The congregation won high commendation from the American Baptist Home Mission Societies in 1968 as "one of the most decisive pioneering church groups in America." Judson's "unique educational and servant ministries" [1] have led the people of the church from tradition to mission and are tangible signs of the congregation's dealing with the urban setting.

NOTES

[1] Quoted from *The Judson Messenger.*

4

JUDSON MEMORIAL CHURCH IN GREENWICH VILLAGE

It would be hard to imagine two churches with greater contrasts than Judson Memorial Church in Minneapolis and Judson Memorial Church in New York's Greenwich Village. Both are named in honor of Adoniram Judson, pioneer Baptist missionary to Burma; and both have creative services of worship, a streamlined church organization, two full-time ministers, and members who represent all the major denominations. For each church the realities of its situation are major factors in determining the shape of its ministry.

Beyond such surface similarities, the contrasts are startling. Judson in Minneapolis has a membership of 500 in a city of 500,000 people, and Judson in the Village has 140 members in a city with eight million people. Yet, because of its outstanding programs in the creative arts and community service, the Village church is far more widely known than its Minneapolis counterpart.

The Minneapolis congregation is made up largely of families and teenagers and includes perhaps a dozen artists. The community has political stability and widespread ecumenical involvement. The nearest university campus is almost ten miles from the church.

In the Village congregation, well-educated young adults greatly outnumber families. Seventy-five percent work for nonprofit institutions; sixteen are ordained ministers. Judson Memorial is dually related to the American Baptist Convention and the United Church of Christ.

The community includes a high concentration of talented artists in all fields. The nearest university campus, New York University with 35,000 students, is about ten yards from the church boundaries. Since New York is still recovering from the days of Tammany Hall, political involvement is extremely important.

Judson in the Village has been called "far-out" so often one wonders if it is on the moon. Actually, it is a large, yellow brick structure facing Washington Square Arch and surrounded by a curious combination of luxurious high-rise apartments, old brownstones, quiet mews where famous writers once lived, the student dormitories of N.Y.U., and the cold-water flats of the East Village. Non-churchgoers dominate the community; most of the nice ladies in Sunday hats have fled to the suburbs or gone to their Maker.

Judson's minister, Dr. Howard R. Moody, believes that this church's role is to be a happening in the midst of the world. Unsure of what the consequences will be, its members carry on their somewhat hesitant pilgrimage, exploring what it means to be the church in an urban setting. The members of this church see their role as that of servants to those in need, not as recruiters for a heavenly kingdom. They believe the world must write the agenda for Judson's programs.

The last thing anyone at Judson would suggest is that it be adopted as a model for churches in general. Because Judson doesn't serve all people's needs, it senses little competition with the traditional congregations of the Village. Many feel that it has deliberately chosen to direct its attention to those outside the church rather than to those who have been comfortable for decades within the church's life.

WORLDLY WORSHIP

Judson's search for its identity began in 1949 under the leadership of the late Dr. Robert Spike. Together, minister and lay people sought to determine their orientation to the surrounding community and to recover a theologically sound basis of worship which was faithful to the heritage of the free church tradition. Their pilgrimage took many paths: conducting a study group on Kierkegaard in a Village coffee house; standing in court with a teenage delinquent; and sponsoring an exhibit of Rouault's paintings. The idea of a dialogue between the church and the world became increasingly essential in the minds of the members.

After intensive study by the congregation, a rich service of worship evolved which was based largely on the *Book of Common Order* of the Church of Scotland. It included reading the gospel, singing hymns, offering prayers, and preaching a sermon.

When Howard Moody became the senior minister in 1956, he continued the same pattern, insisting that this heritage of worship was a necessary balance for the far-out activities in which Judson members engaged during the rest of the week. Finally, when growing numbers of the congregation insisted with equal vehemence that they could not understand why their dance concerts and theater happenings were so much more exciting than their worship services, they realized that further study was needed. A twelve-member worship committee was appointed in 1965, including church board members, painters, playwrights, dancers, actors, and musicians. They met for four hours each week for a full year, struggling to answer the twin questions of how Judson's worship could reflect its involvement in social action and the arts and how worship could include the sorrows and joys of urban life.

Although visitors are sometimes disturbed by what they see on a Sunday morning, Judson members have enough openness, freedom, and insight into the underlying purposes to give an enthusiastic welcome to the creative experimentation in worship. Dance, drama, multi-media presentations, paintings, and jazz have all been explored as avenues of worship. When there is a sermon, it is likely to be topical, intellectual, and directly to the point.

Two basic traditions from the heritage of the Christian church remain as a central part of Judson's worship. Every service involves the reading of the Word. The Lord's Supper is observed on the first Sunday of each month in a meal which reminds the worshiping congregation of what brings them together. On communion Sundays, the meal shapes the liturgy. Tables are set up all over the meeting room. As the congregation shares French bread and wine, fruit and cheese, they sing together and talk of their deep concerns.

One of the major conclusions of the worship committee was that the best definition of worship is found in Romans: "Present your bodies as a living sacrifice, . . . which is your reasonable service" (12:1, KJV). After much thought, this indicated that life itself was the real act of worship and that the cultic act is merely a reminder of, or a pointer to, what the real act of worship is.

Dr. Moody summed it up on a 1969 telecast when he said, "The meeting room is made holy not by incense or by prayers, but by the actions of its people."

Special Sundays are given special treatment. One Palm Sunday the choir and organ were replaced by a jazz trio and a dance group in white leotards. The following year, when some visitors arrived at 11 A.M. for the Easter Sunday service, they found a note on the door indicating that Easter had been celebrated at 5 A.M. with a happening in Washington Square Park!

Sometimes a service of mixed media is used for shock therapy. On Race Relations Sunday in 1968, the congregation listened to a tape recording of a sermon by the late Malcolm X on "Bullets or Ballots." Simultaneously, they watched slides of "America the Beautiful" on one screen and a silent color film of the 1967 Newark riots on the second screen. The walls around the meeting room were hung with graphic photos portraying the last ten years of race relations in this nation.

In a seminar Dr. Moody explained: "Liberation and celebration are the goals of what happens to people in Judson worship. Worship helps us become freer persons and gives us an opportunity to say thanks and alleluia for what happens to us. Tears and laughter have a place in worship, too."

Worship at Judson is subject to probing by people who demand that symbols mean something, that language say something, that liturgy be alive. As a handmaiden of theology, the arts provide tools and methods for experiences in worship that bridge the incredible gap between liturgy and life. This wedding of faith and art may help men find new methods of celebrating the judgment and presence of God.

FAITH AND ART

"The artist is an important barometer of what's happening to us as a people," Howard Moody has explained. "Our first role is one of listening and looking, with an openness of mind and heart. Our second task is affirmation."

He elaborated this point further in an article in *Renewal Magazine:*

> We no longer have to read a religious commercial in every poem or see a "holy vision" in every painting. We can enjoy art for its own revelation of terror or beauty which it brings to our life. We can "swing" with and appreciate jazz without explaining its religious origins.
> . . . It is enough if there shines through art, in all its forms, the mystery and creativity that brought it into being.[1]

Daniel Wolf, publisher of the *Village Voice,* declared: "Judson opened a pipeline between the avant-garde and the more conventional society of the Village." [2] This pipeline follows four major channels: the Judson Poets' Theatre, the Judson Gallery, the Judson Dance Theatre, and the Chamber Music Program.

Founded in 1961, the Judson Poets' Theatre has become one of the most vital forces in "Off-Off Broadway" theater. Some of its enthusiasts believe it has attracted talent which has contributed more to the world of the theater than has the Repertory Theatre of Lincoln Center with all of its plush luxury.

Judson has won eleven "Obie" awards, the Off-Broadway equivalent of Oscars, and five productions have graduated to commercial runs in Off-Broadway theaters since 1964. One of these was *In Circles* by Gertrude Stein, directed by Lawrence Kornfeld, and featuring music by Al Carmines, assistant minister at Judson. It received a rave review from Clive Barnes of the *New York Times;* and Jack Kroll of *Newsweek* wrote, "The Judson Poets' Theatre performs Gertrude Stein the way the Moscow Art Theatre does Chekov." [3]

Judson's earliest venture into the arts was the founding of the Judson Gallery in 1957. Its Quaker director, John Hendricks, says, "Programs like ours wouldn't be relevant in most communities, because most churches don't live where the artists live." The Gallery gave Pop Art masters Claes Oldenburg, Jim Dine, and others their first New York showings. [4]

The Judson Dance Theatre was launched in 1962, largely through the encouragement of Robert Rauschenberg, who is both a painter and choreographer. Today, Judson has the leading avant-garde dance center in New York and presents up to thirty programs a year. [5]

Ed Brewer, the full-time organist and choirmaster, initiated the Chamber Music Program in 1964. It not only provides music for the worship services but also presents late Sunday afternoon concerts that range from Bach to Bartok.

The Judson drama program has a large and faithful following that turns out for every show, even if it receives an unfavorable review in the *Village Voice*. Some plays are given in the choir loft, which seats one hundred, and others in the meeting room, which seats three hundred. No matter where or when the show is given, some people are turned away.

The Judson theater creates an excitement in its audience. As a front-page story in the theater section of the *New York Times* indicated: "They emerge from the warmth and intimacy of the choir loft or the open freedom of the meeting room with the glow of people who have struck a heady, if somewhat unfocused, blow for freedom." [6]

POLITICS AND PROTEST

Creative worship and a platform for the arts are not the only distinctives of Judson Church. It has also been enormously active in political life and in protest demonstrations for peace, civil rights, and free speech.

For more than a decade Howard Moody has been a pillar of the reform movement in New York City's Democratic Party, which finally unseated the leadership of Tammany Hall. He was co-chairman of Democrats for Lindsay in 1965; and during the first political rally held in the new Madison Square Garden, he led a fund appeal for presidential candidate Eugene McCarthy, which raised $300,000 from twenty thousand people.

Long active in the civil rights movement, Dr. Moody represented the congregation at Selma and was arrested for blocking the path of a cement truck during an integration demonstration in Brooklyn.

Judsonites protested for five weeks to gain removal of a ban on folk singers in Washington Square Park. They have also fought City Hall on many other issues: to keep the Village safe from an extension of Fifth Avenue, safe from high-rise apartments, safe for coffee houses, and safe for people of every color, creed, and sex who live there. Judson sponsored pioneer clinics for drug addicts and took part in a protest at City Hall demanding that the city provide the necessary funds for narcotics clinics.

On behalf of thirty-one other ministers and rabbis, Dr. Moody administers an agency that deals with the issues presented by problem pregnancies, the Clergy Consultation Service on Abortion. In its first five months of operation, they interviewed over eight hundred women with problem pregnancies. Insisting that reform legislation on abortion must be adopted, he wrote in *Glamour* magazine, "The only difference between *legal* and *illegal* abortions in New York is money and whom you know." [7]

One of the keys to Judson's effectiveness is its ability to listen to what people are saying. This openness was perhaps best demonstrated during the year the church sponsored the "Hall of Issues."

Begun at the suggestion of a young artist, it gave any artist or writer who felt a deep-seated protest a chance to exhibit in the church hall a literary or artistic form embodying the protest and then defend it before a group of his peers. Between 100 and 150 people attended nearly every session. Often those in attendance witnessed the incongruity of a beatnik artist arguing out his protest with another type of Greenwich Villager—a Wall Street lawyer or an associate editor of *Life*.

Howard Moody feels that the minister as change-agent in the church today has a choice of three roles. The reformer advocates liberalizing laws and practices so that they are not so hard to obey. The revolutionist may say that the whole system is wrong and must be destroyed, although the new system he proposes may result in a new enslavement. The radical, on the other hand, looks at the roots of the problem to see what reason prompted the law or practice and whether it is still valid.

Anyone studying Judson Church in Greenwich Village would probably conclude that it belongs in the radical category—and that perhaps the radical approach is the most reasonable answer to the problem of achieving renewal within the church. Churches that dare to let God break through in new ways can maintain the essentials and dispense with the trivia.

NOTES

[1] Howard Moody, "Toward a Religionless Church for a Secular World," reprinted from *Renewal Magazine* in Stephen C. Rose, ed., *Who's Killing the Church?* (Chicago: Association Press, 1966), p. 88.

[2] *New York Times Magazine,* June 6, 1965, p. 116.

[3] Frederick G. Myers, Jr., "Judson: An Encounter with the Arts," *United Church Herald,* Division of Publications of the United Church Board for Homeland Ministries, April 1968, p. 18.

[4] *Ibid.*

[5] *Ibid.*

[6] Elenore Lester, "In the Parish Hall, the Hippies Go Ape," *New York Times,* March 26, 1967, p. 3.

[7] Howard Moody, "Protest," *Glamour,* April, 1968, p. 38.

5

ST. PETER'S LUTHERAN
CHURCH IN MANHATTAN

Some of Duke Ellington's best friends are clergymen. Near the top of the list he would put Dr. John G. Gensel, minister to New York's jazz community and a staff member of St. Peter's Lutheran Church. He encouraged the Duke's interest in composing sacred music in the jazz idiom and spearheaded the planning for Mr. Ellington's momentous concert at Fifth Avenue Presbyterian Church in 1965. Two performances were heard by four thousand people, and they considered it the religious event of the season. Three years later 7,500 people heard a second concert at the Cathedral Church of St. John the Divine.

When Duke Ellington was growing up in Washington, D.C., he went to church twice every Sunday—to the Baptist church with his mother and the Methodist service with his father. By 1923 he was leading his own jazz group, and later *Swing* magazine noted that the Duke composed seventeen of the twenty-eight hit tunes of 1940. His first sacred concert, at Grace Cathedral in San Francisco, quickly made history. Pleased to have clergymen accept him on the team, he explained, "Now I can say loudly and openly what I have been saying to myself on my knees." [1] To express his gratitude, the Duke brought Pastor Gensel a gold New Testament from Jerusalem and enjoyed having Dr. and Mrs. Gensel at his seventieth birthday dinner at the White House.

John Gensel's interest in jazz began in 1931 in Berwick, Pennsylvania, when he heard a concert by Duke Ellington. The teenager sensed immediately that this music was a language that spoke to his own deep needs. For months he spent his evenings logging the music played by jazz bands he heard in person, over the radio, or on recordings. After graduating from college and seminary, he was a navy chaplain on Guam; and he served churches in Ohio, as well as in San Juan in his native Puerto Rico. In 1956 he came to New York City as pastor of Advent Lutheran Church.

Excited by reading *The Story of Jazz* by Professor Marshall Stearns, he visited the author in Greenwich Village and enrolled in his course on the influence of jazz at the New School for Social Research. Class assignments included lecture tours of jazz clubs like Cafe Bohemia and the Village Gate, and introductions to jazz musicians. When the course ended, Pastor Gensel and his wife Audrey continued going to the jazz spots to hear the musicians he had met.

One night a jazzman came to his table saying, "Pastor, I'd like to talk with you." The hour-long conversation which followed could have been heard in any pastor's study, but the setting was far different. One musician told another, and before long the Lutheran minister found himself spending more and more evenings listening to the music and the problems of jazz musicians. Without even trying to do something unusual, he suddenly realized his pastoral concern had propelled him into conducting a night ministry, the first in the nation.[2]

The difficulty was that he was also pastor of Advent Lutheran Church! When he had arrived, the church had been without a minister for a year. He had to work hard to build the church to two hundred active members. Now he found he couldn't be out three or four nights a week until 3 A.M. and still administer a congregation. Encouraged by Professor Stearns, Dr. Luther Cloud, and Ruth Ellington, the Duke's sister, Dr. Gensel was freed for this ministry. The Lutheran Board of American Missions provided the church with a full-time assistant minister in 1960; and in 1965 it was agreed to have John Gensel serve the jazz community full time in a five-year experiment. When Ralph E. Peterson became the preaching minister at St. Peter's in 1966, Dr. Gensel moved the headquarters of his jazz ministry there.

THE JAZZ PASTOR

The jazz ministry has three major emphases. To Dr. Gensel, the most significant is his pastoral care for musicians and their families. He laughs and says, "I don't play a note, but I'm a good listener." He listens to the rhythm with all the appreciation of a jazz buff and concentrates as a pastor on the words jazzmen murmur to him during performance breaks. An old-timer suggested that he befriend the bartenders since they usually knew who was sick or in trouble. He probably knows more bartenders than any other teetotaler in New York. Because John Gensel takes the initiative in going to the places where jazzmen are and quietly makes his presence known by wearing his clerical collar, the musicians recognize him as a friend and come to him when they feel the need of help.

Usually what they want most is a sympathetic ear. Sometimes they need a minister to speak on their behalf to the immigration authorities or to union officials. He is invited to special occasions, including a benefit for the widow of Malcolm X at the estate of Mrs. Sidney Poitier. He conducts weddings and funerals and visits musicians who are hospitalized. At the funeral for Billy Strayhorn, composer of *Take the A Train,* sleek black limousines brought to St. Peter's a long line of celebrities, including Duke Ellington, Lena Horne, Benny Goodman, and Jackie Robinson.

The second emphasis of this ministry, jazz vespers at St. Peter's at five o'clock every Sunday afternoon, may be the most distinctive element. A decade ago both jazzmen and churchmen felt jazz and religion occupied separate worlds. After some trial and error in early attempts to wed the two, Pastor Gensel discovered "Jazz is improvisatory by its nature, and when it is played for worship it becomes a prayer, a cry of loneliness, a shout of joy." [3]

For urban man, Bach and Haydn may not be synonyms for divinity. Jazz is fresh and realistic, pulsing with the urgency of today. It speaks of a world filled with problems and yet it is an affirmation of life. The listener is challenged to ponder the imponderables—as his foot taps, his lips move, and his whole being responds. In John Gensel's opinion, "This is the way we should be involved in worship. We're using music of today just as Luther and Wesley used the music of their day."

More than one hundred musicians a year take part in the jazz vespers, often composing special music for the occasion. Performers include pianists Eddie Bonnémere and Roger Kellaway, folksinger Robert Edwin, trumpeter Howard McGhee, the Joe Newman Quintet, the Manhattan Brass Choir, and many others.

Congregations average 115 persons, with up to seven hundred people crowding the sanctuary for special events. A jazz prelude and a call to worship precede a congregational prayer expressed in simple, modern language:

People: Forgive us, God,
We're stubborn fools and liars—
dishonest even with ourselves.
We don't love others
We war against life
We hurt each other
All of us are human, and yet we
won't admit the limitations of
our humanity.
We're sorry for it, and we're sick
of it.
We need a new way of living.

Pastor: Giver of life, help us—heal us!

People: Spirit of God, speak to us and help
us to listen.
You know we're very deaf
Make these moments full.

Continuing the worship service, Pastor Gensel introduces the guest musicians explaining:

> Each of the musicians here today has been given a special gift—a talent for music. This music is so much a part of their lives that it says what their words often can't—about happiness, sadness and faith. Today they are offering their music to say what they feel about their God.

Lively anthems or stirring solos may receive spontaneous applause, which does not seem inappropriate even in a Gothic sanctuary. Following the sermon there is a brief discussion on the "issue of the week." This covers topics as varied as Vietnam, LSD, the Black Manifesto, or the New York teachers' strike. A rousing postlude echoes the final line of the benediction, "Go, serve the Lord. You are free!"

Eddie Bonnémere, a Catholic music teacher and jazz pianist born in Harlem, composed a contemporary Lutheran liturgy to express his appreciation for this ministry. In a news release he declared: "At St. Peter's, you feel you belong. It's like a dialogue. A musician can be himself and there is a great sense of openness."

Bridge-building is the third emphasis, and perhaps the one with the greatest permanent value in John Gensel's ministry. He attempts to narrow the communications gap between jazz-lovers and society at large, especially where jazz and religion are concerned. His schedule includes many lectures on college and seminary campuses and frequent appearances as a panelist on local and network broadcasts. He often guides groups of students or laymen on visits to New York jazz spots. On a fall weekend in 1968 he presided at the Eastern Conference of Jazz Societies, which brought four hundred participants to St. Peter's for lectures, panel discussions, and plenty of music.

At least once a year John Gensel gets involved in planning special performances for large audiences. The sacred concert by Duke Ellington at Fifth Avenue Presbyterian in 1965 was followed by a jazz worship service in 1966 at the Newport Jazz Festival, and a concert at Carnegie Hall entitled "Praise the Lord in Many Voices." Programs at Town Hall in May, 1967, and March, 1969, featured selections composed by musicians who have worked closely with the jazz ministry.

AN AVANT-GARDE CHURCH

Jazz vespers are not the only attractions that draw the long-haired and miniskirted to St. Peter's. They are attracted by relevant sermons preached by Ralph Peterson and by the dramatic performances at St. Peter's Gate. Its Theatre-at-Noon attracts the bag-lunch crowd from nearby skyscrapers and specialty stores, offering them satire and brief dramas in a mood which is different from either secular skepticism or churchy gush. "St. Peter's is probably the only Lutheran congregation in the country where the clergy and young adults can be seen walking to a nearby tavern after services on Sunday for Bloody Marys, Eggs Benedict, and theological discussion." [4]

Just as St. Peter's 1905 Gothic spires are in vivid contrast to the steel and glass skyscrapers that dwarf it, so its program is an unusual blend of the traditional and the experimental. On the traditional side, it serves holy communion six days a week. Its leaders realize that "the love of God must be communicated not only in the language of jazz, but also in the language of the lonely office girl, the young executive, the visiting U.N. aide, the retired life-long member." [5]

St. Peter's serves three distinct congregations. It has its official members, the business and professional people who work nearby during the week, and a large group of Sunday visitors. This three-dimensional constituency has helped to shape the church's program.

Even its educational ministry is avant-garde. Forty children and their leaders conduct their own mini-service and take field trips to Chinatown, a synagogue, a Lutheran college, or an ocean liner! With so much going on, it's small wonder that seminaries are eager to study this church at close range. In 1968 it had fifteen seminarians, who also participated in action training and sensitivity programs directed by MUST, the ecumenical Metropolitan Urban Service Training program.

Significantly, most of the members of St. Peter's are involved in the work of the church. They believe that they must give of themselves to others if the presence of the living God is to be made known by his people to his world.

NOTES

[1] *New York Times,* January 16, 1968, p. 26.

[2] Stanley G. Matthews, *The Night Pastors* (New York: Hawthorn Books, Inc., 1967), pp. 16-30. Copyright 1967 by Stanley G. Matthews. Price $4.95. Published by Hawthorn Books, Inc., 70 Fifth Avenue, New York, New York.

[3] James A. Lokken, "Blues for Billy Strayhorn," *Lutheran Forum,* August, 1967. Copyright 1967 by American Lutheran Publicity Bureau.

[4] *Ibid.*

[5] *Ibid.*

6

SECOND BAPTIST CHURCH IN LOS ANGELES

In Los Angeles, Second Baptist is trying hard to be a Christian church. Nobody claims the goal has been reached. Its members are hung up with old forms but are willing to try new ones. They know the inertia of eighty-five years and occasionally discover the buoyancy of the sixteen-year-old. They try harder than most churches to bridge the gaps between generations, races, and theologies. Second Baptist is a servant church in action, alert to the winds of change. It seeks to find where God is working in the world and where he is going.[1]

In many ways, Second Baptist is a traditional congregation. It has two worship services each Sunday morning, a midweek prayer service, an annual school of missions, and extensive programs in Christian education and evangelism.

But Second Baptist is not content to do only the traditional things. It recognizes that its resources make it one of the pace-setting churches in California. Its group of buildings form a million-dollar complex, and its annual budget is $256,000. A majority of its 2200 members represents a broad cross section of black society in Los Angeles. In 1969 its senior minister, Dr. Thomas Kilgore, became the first black president of the American Baptist Convention. Although Second Baptist has never split, it has become the mother of three hundred other black churches in southern California since its founding in 1885.

To an unusual degree, each member sees himself as one of the 2200 ministers of Second Baptist. They have come to understand that they *are* change-agents in the church and in the world. They take with great seriousness Dr. Kilgore's definition of the church as that company of believers where Jesus Christ is Lord of the church and the world, where the real ministry is the ministry of the

laity, and where the nature of the church is to be the servant people of a servant God.[2]

THE WINDS OF CHANGE

One of this church's innovations has been to call to its staff a
young minister who happens to be white. Ellis M. Keck is a 1969
graduate of the American Baptist Seminary of the West. During his
seminary years he was a student assistant at Second Baptist
Church, and he gained so much from working with the people
that he quickly accepted the invitation to become the full-time
pastor of youth and visitation.

Mr. Keck has noted some clear-cut differences between worship
services in white churches and in black churches. In an interview
he explained: "Whites are quick to express joy at the ballgame
but usually feel joy is out of place in the sanctuary. Black churches
have more charisma and spontaneity. Dr. Kilgore's sermons reflect
some of the best theology in the books as well as a lively awareness of the spirit of God. Our pulpit prayers are intensely personal,
and we find that the black worshiper is a real participant, not a
bystander."

The woman's society is one of the areas where the winds of
change have been felt. The women at Second Baptist have declared that they want more than "White Cross package" involvement with mission fields. Program content has become more contemporary, and there is a stronger accent on service. One circle
makes Easter clothes for neighbors in need, and a young women's
group has "adopted" a family of eleven. They sew school clothes
for the girls and buy them for the boys. The circles usually gather
in members' homes, but occasionally they meet at Baptist-related
institutions or with white churches in suburbia. They sometimes
even hold their programs in soul-food restaurants!

Youth have become deeply involved in the life of the church.
In addition to participating in youth fellowships and church school
classes, they serve on the official boards, have a youth choir that
sings the second Sunday of each month, enlist a youth board of
ushers, and present special programs for the whole church. In
1969 these programs included an original drama during Easter
week, a creative worship service for the annual music festival,
production of a motion picture, and sponsorship of a weekend
conference on war, peace, and racism.

Mr. Keck said: "Black young people are doing their own think-ing and reject many old patterns held by both white and black adults. This is especially true when they consider the new morality. My sex ethics were hammered out when I was between eighteen and twenty-five. Today black kids have to face these questions when they are ten or twelve! They are intensely concerned about being human and about having a marriage relationship that will be enduring, yet not one motivated by taboos. Under the old morality, decisions were made for you. The rules said, 'Thou shalt not,' and that was that. In the new morality you think it through for your-self and act out of love, not duty."

COMMITTED TO SERVE ITS COMMUNITY

The greatest area of change since Dr. Kilgore became pastor in 1963 has been for Second Baptist to broaden its involvement in community life. Its strong membership and excellent physical facilities have a strategic location, on the edge of Watts, in an area of downtown Los Angeles that is on the verge of becoming a black ghetto. Because of its size and location the church is visited by a steady stream of newcomers from the Mississippi delta and else-where who seek help to find jobs, housing, food, and spiritual nur-ture.

The first steps in meeting community needs were taken cau-tiously. Dr. Kilgore persuaded the congregation to reactivate the Henderson Community Center next door to the church. It has become the headquarters for five adult-education classes taught in cooperation with the Los Angeles school system. The church also sponsors the Storehouse which gives away canned goods and cloth-ing to hundreds of residents and newcomers to the city. Also, two paid workers staff the Teen Post year-round, from 3 P.M. to 9 P.M. Its two hundred participants include school dropouts who have police records, drug addicts, and those with agonizing family prob-lems.

Second Baptist moved into high gear on community involvement at the time of the Watts riot in August, 1965. On the day the riot began, Dr. Kilgore was in Birmingham, Alabama, attending the annual meeting of the Southern Christian Leadership Conference and picketing the courthouse to protest the lack of blacks in gov-ernment jobs. When he heard a news flash about the Watts riot, he decided he was marching in the wrong place and caught the next plane back to Los Angeles. The riot not only scarred the church neighborhood but jarred the conviction held by many members of Second that they were already living up to their responsibilities for their neighbors.

Shortly after the riot Dr. Kilgore led a group of people, mostly clergymen, to talk with the publisher of the *Los Angeles Times* about the role which that powerful newspaper had in the community. Despite initial opposition, the paper began to change its stance on handling news affecting black people. It even changed some of its editorial policies and agreed to run feature stories on outstanding black leaders and families.

Planning also began for a 60-unit apartment complex to be built by Second Baptist, using the American Baptist Service Corporation as adviser. Thirty units will be used for senior citizens and thirty for general housing, as a form of ministry to the community surrounding the church.

One of Second's most ambitious achievements is the Child Development Center. It is the first federally funded child-care training center established under Title IV of the Economic Opportunities Act and receives a federal grant of $190,000 per year, plus county funds. Under the direction of Mrs. Kilgore and a staff of twenty-five, it cares for 125 children from 6 A.M. to 6 P.M. The program is especially structured for children who are emotionally, culturally, or educationally deprived. Its goal is to free the parents of welfare children to receive adequate training and hopefully to escape the welfare rolls.

Second Baptist is often the catalyst that brings about change. When the local branch of the NAACP appeared to be lacking in strength, the ministers and the congregation enlisted fifteen hundred new members for the NAACP. This move gave them a strong position in the organization. In April, 1968, Dr. Kilgore was one of the founders of MATE (Mutual Assistance Team Endeavor), which brought together black pastors and staff members of the Baptist city society and state convention. It matched ten inner-city and suburban churches to carry out joint projects that affect white racism, poverty, and inadequate education. Judge Albert Matthews, a member of Second, chairs the MATE board.

The Pueblo Christian Action Center was organized in cooperation with the American Baptist Home Mission Societies and the city mission society. Second Baptist took over a building which was once a liquor store and hired skilled workmen from the congregation to do the renovations. All kinds of things are happening there: citizenship classes, youth and adult clubs, family counseling, community organization, health and welfare services, films, referrals, Christian education, and tutoring. Some of the participants are school dropouts, some are prostitutes, and some are involved with narcotics.

The center director, C. J. Malloy, kept working with one young fellow who had been a drug peddler until he got him a job. The young man had been making as much as $500 a week on drugs, and now he earns $3.53 an hour. One evening he came in and told the director, "You know I am not making as much money, but I feel a lot better. Now I don't have to keep looking over my shoulder to see who is coming after me."

The sanctuary of Second Baptist has become a kind of city auditorium for many community groups, including some black militants. Perhaps the most notable occasion was Thanksgiving weekend in 1966, when nine hundred young people from nine states attended the Black Youth Congress. Because a similar conference in Newark had involved confrontation, nobody else in Los Angeles would have them. When Dr. Kilgore called the trustees, all except one agreed to let these young people use Second Baptist.

Certain ground rules were worked out, including the presence of staff members. Dr. Kilgore welcomed the group, and they gave him thirty minutes to talk about the power and relevancy of the church and the fact that many of them had "copped out." His forthright statement and the openness of the church toward them must have prompted some second thoughts about writing off the church altogether! In an address at Green Lake, Wisconsin, Dr. Kilgore said:

> I think that it is because this one church first opened the door to these young people to say to them "We care about you, we believe you are God's children like everybody else." We knew they had hang-ups but we also knew we had hang-ups. Therefore, we were not afraid to enter into conversation with them. And there have been many, many other excellent relationships with these young people, alienated from the church and everybody else, simply because the church was not afraid to make the first step.[3]

Dr. Kilgore is generally credited with a major role in helping

Los Angeles stay on an even keel when news came of the assassination of Dr. Martin Luther King, Jr., one of his close personal friends. Enough rapport had already been established so that he could bring together ministers and black militants for a day-long strategy session at Second Baptist. A hundred cities across the nation experienced violence, but in the powder keg of Los Angeles, police reports for that weekend showed less violence than usual. Instead, eighteen hundred people packed Second Baptist Friday night, and sixteen thousand came to a city-wide memorial service on Sunday. On Friday night one of the featured speakers was a black preacher and the other was a black militant. Dr. Kilgore commented later in an address: "We have tried to have revivals at Second Baptist . . . but I have never seen one in which there was more spirit than that night. . . . caught up in the wake of a terrible tragedy . . . we needed some guidance that was beyond us." [4]

Ministers and members of Second Baptist have been unusually active in political campaigns for the president and the mayor. They involved eighty churches in the crisis over the public schools in Los Angeles. Such activities are seen as part of the task of the servant church. In Dr. Kilgore's words: "God is in the world as well as in the church." [5]

NOTES

[1] From "The Current Story of an Inner City Church," a mimeographed report prepared by Second Baptist Church, Los Angeles, in 1969.

[2] From an address by Dr. Thomas Kilgore, Jr., at the Conference on the Church, American Baptist Assembly, Green Lake, Wisconsin, August 5, 1969, p. 3.

[3] *Ibid.*

[4] *Ibid.*

[5] *Ibid.*

7

THE CHURCH OF THE SAVIOUR
IN WASHINGTON, D. C.

Most congregations are about as easy to join as the Book-of-the-Month Club. But this is not true of the Church of the Saviour, which has its headquarters in a 25-room brownstone on Embassy Row in Washington, D.C., and is one of the few churches in the nation to be categorized by the Yellow Pages as an ecumenical church.

Most boards of deacons would quake at the Church of the Saviour's definition of a minimum discipline for church membership: completion of five courses in the School of Christian Living; preparation of a detailed paper on Christian living; six weeks of preparation under the guidance of a sponsor; study of the church constitution and memorization of the covenant of membership, renewed annually, which is as follows:

> We covenant with Christ and one another to:
> Meet God daily in a set time of prayer
> Let God confront us daily through the Scriptures
> Grow in love for the brotherhood and for all people. . . .
> Worship weekly—normally with our church
> Be a vital contributing member of one of the groups
> Give proportionately, beginning at a tithe of our incomes
> Confess and ask the help of our fellowship should we fail
> in these expressions of devotion[1]

The Church of the Saviour is closer to "being the church" than any other group I have encountered. The demanding requirements for membership probably explain why this church is still creative, rather than traditional, after twenty years.

A good capsule definition of their pilgrimage is found in a paragraph of Elizabeth O'Connor's book *Call to Commitment:*

> The Church of the Saviour is an attempt to recover in one local

expression of the Church Universal something of the vitality and life, vigor and power of the early Christian community. It was founded on the conviction that the greatest contribution the church can make in any time is in being the church—"a fellowship of reconciled and reconciling men," a community of the Holy Spirit, a people in which Christ dwells, a people who have a newness of life and who are transmitters of this newness.[2]

Founded in 1947, the Church of the Saviour cannot be described in terms of impressive membership statistics (they have seventy members and more than one hundred active participants); a thundering pipe organ (they use a second-hand piano); or the loftiness of their steeple (brownstones don't come with steeples). Allowed only three words to summarize their pilgrimage, I would choose *discipline, community,* and *mission.*

DISCIPLINE

Discipline is woven into the very fabric of this church. In one sermon, their pastor Gordon Cosby said that discipline is harder for a congregation which attempts to take commitment seriously: "The shape of the people of God is a praying people, a worshiping people who give time and tithes as an expression of love and who take seriously their mission to the world. In one sense, a person's entrance into the kingdom of God depends upon belonging to a disciplined people. There is a terrible scarcity of people who have let God take root in their lives at a depth level. We need people with a charismatic character around whom other people can adhere."

He concluded: "Discipline involves pressure to help us be open at the places where we hurt." For example, during a ten-minute period of silent meditation in the worship service, members of the congregation were asked to think through their present disciplines, ponder the possibilities of adopting new ones if they were ready for them, and then to write down a list, sign and date it, begin following the new disciplines that day, and tell their decisions to some other member of the congregation.

One of the most effective ways discovered by the Church of the Saviour to practice and strengthen these disciplines is for one church member to develop a relationship with another church member who serves as one's "spiritual director" for a period of three months, a year, or longer. In a relationship of openness and trust, one reveals one's hidden self, doubts, and fears and receives help to grow in Christ.

COMMUNITY

The most important aspect of the Church of the Saviour is that it involves both the *gathered* fellowship and the *dispersed* witnesses. Christians are called by God to be and to act, not endlessly to discuss. The depth experiences of the inward journey compel the witness and service which mark the outward journey. The need for both kinds of experience is maintained even when "those who are eager for mission and have been attracted by the church's involvement in the city fight the disciplined devotional life" or when "others who are attracted by the opportunity to grow in the life of prayer and worship look askance at coffee houses and freedom walks." [3]

When a new member joins the fellowship of the church, he is brought immediately into a small group where he can receive and contribute fellowship at the *koinonia* level. Every church should establish this kind of group that really grapples with the issues of the Christian faith and where the members grow sufficiently in Christian love and understanding that they will dare to be open with each other, dropping their masks and experiencing the joy that comes from not having to pretend anymore.

The membership of the Church of the Saviour is widely varied. When a visitor asked an usher if he were a charter member, he replied, "Not quite, because I was in jail then." There are doctors and teachers, sales clerks and barbers, high government officials, a sculptress, maids, and television broadcasters.

One of Gordon Cosby's firm beliefs is that the church cannot preach a message and then leave people to work out its implications by themselves. Within the life of the church, people must find concrete help in facing the problems of the worlds in which they live—the worlds of work, of family, of politics, of education. This process begins with the educational ministry of the church, which centers in the School of Christian Living.

Courses are taught on a quarterly basis, each lasting about three months. Required subjects include Old Testament, New Testament, Doctrine, Christian Community, and Christian Growth. Reading assignments are on a college level in Bonhoeffer, Brunner, Robert McAfee Brown, C. H. Dodd, John Casteel, J. B. Phillips, J. S.

Whale, and Paul Tournier. Each course is planned to lead to that most decisive of all choices: total commitment to Christ.

The philosophy of education for church members is explained succinctly in *Call to Commitment*. They do not exclude from the Christian community a person who has not attended classes. Membership is simply a means by which to define his participation in the mission. "We do not ask him to articulate what he does not know, or subject him to pressures for which he is not ready." [4]

As an air force chaplain who endured the Battle of the Bulge, Gordon Cosby saw enough of what stress could do to even active church members to be convinced that merely paper church membership was not enough. He was determined to organize a church based on the convictions which he had hammered out in the face of death.

He believes the primary task of the professional minister is that of training nonprofessional ministers for the ministry. Rather than adopting the role of the authoritarian clergyman, he prefers to be an enabler, to take the shape of a servant who bends himself to another's need and who releases, trains, and directs the gifts of the Holy Spirit, which are then poured into the congregation's life. At the same time, he leads when leading is necessary. He minces no words in the pulpit. One of his parishioners said, "One reason Gordon is on target so often in his sermons is because of the depth of his own prayer life."

MISSION

For those who yearn for a vital Christianity, the Church of the Saviour is the place to be. Quaker theologian Elton Trueblood has remarked that the level of concern and outreach there "makes most of us ashamed of our mild Christianity." [5]

Being "on mission" in the world is part of the commitment of each member. They point out frequently that the polished brass plaque on their Massachusetts Avenue brownstone declares that the building is the *"headquarters* of the Church of the Saviour." (Italics added.) They are firmly convinced that wherever they are in the world, there is the church. This belief is not just a matter of "church people at work in the world," but rather that *they are the church in the world,* a far different thing.

Elizabeth O'Connor wrote in her second book, *Journey Inward, Journey Outward:*

For us the structures to hold the inward and the outward became what we call our mission groups. In these mission groups the Church of the Saviour finds its shape. Each group has the disciplines essential for the engagement with self and God and others, and each has those peculiar disciplines for the servant task.[6]

Part of what it means to be a person in community is to be a person secure enough in love to venture out. The next step for the Christian is that of calling forth the gifts of others and encouraging persons to become more fully human.

Church members are wise enough to recognize that they must not add more people or mission groups than the core can absorb without running a grave risk of spreading themselves so thin that their effectiveness is greatly minimized. Far from following rigid structures, their mission groups change with the needs of times and situations.

The Church of the Saviour's preschool enrichment program was a forerunner of Head Start. It was organized in 1963 to provide cultural enrichment for preschool youngsters of economically deprived families. Based on experimental work by the Institute of Developmental Studies in New York, the Church of the Saviour acted as a catalyst to launch the program by securing the cooperation of many groups. The Washington Center for Metropolitan Studies provided research help; public housing projects gave free space; a professor of psychiatry and his students volunteered skilled teaching aid; and substantial grants came from the Ford Foundation and the United Planning Organization of Washington.

According to a book by John H. Perry, Jr.: "The coffee house epidemic first broke into the clear light of day in 1963, with the publication of *Call to Commitment*. . . ." [7] His study indicated that over one thousand church-sponsored coffee houses came into existence within the next three years. Visitors to the Potter's House in Washington are impressed with the art-lined walls, the skilled use of lighting and music, the exotic coffees, the friendliness of the hostess and waiters, and the "conversation tables" for lonely people. Its visitors include an average of thirty ministers a month.

Initially the Potter's House emphasized dialogue with the arts and dialogue between persons. Its current goal is to achieve a rebuilding of the city of Washington as complete as the recent transformation in Hartford, Connecticut. A flier described the mission in these words:

Since the riots of April, 1968, a sense of hopelessness and pessimism has crept into the public attitude toward the city. The frantic exodus to the suburbs has increased, removing leadership and revenue from the places where it is most sorely needed. Fragmented planning in an attempt to remedy isolated problems has only resulted in bickering and frustration between various government agencies, as well as between them and neighborhood and civic groups. All of this has led to further deterioration and indifference. We at the Potter's House now see our mission as demonstrating to the city that there is a hope and a vision which is within our grasp. The city can be changed and changed now if only we will commit ourselves to the labor and sacrifice which will transform it.[8]

Dialogue about Washington's problems and potential is encouraged through displays, literature, films, and informed speakers and through the serving groups who wait on tables. Members of the mission group have adopted disciplines of prayer and meditation and of an encounter with self. They believe that changing the lives of people is the first step needed in transforming the city.

Other mission groups include one for church school teachers; one that ministers to recent widows; a Renewal Center group that provides a counseling ministry; and a retreat group that operates a center at Dayspring, a two-hundred-acre Maryland farm. The farm also serves as a summer camping area for city children, and half of the weekend retreat dates are used by other churches in the Washington area.

Still another mission group is working with sixteen Washington churches on a project called FLOC (For Love of Children). Their aim is to find foster homes for abandoned and neglected children in Junior Village, an overcrowded welfare institution; and to move the D.C. Welfare Department to develop a sufficient number of group foster homes to replace the present institution.

The federally operated, grossly inadequate Junior Village opened in 1948 with ninety children. By 1958 there were 303 and by 1965 the frightening total of 910. Junior Village represented in microcosm Washington's sore spots in housing, employment, discrimination, disenfranchisement, and welfare legislation. To dramatize the plight of these children to the city, students from Howard University taught the older children to paint, and an art show of their work was held at the Potter's House. The darkness the children had known in their lives came through vividly in their drawings. Even the bright focus of publicity did not budge the regulations, the apathy, or the interwoven economic, social, and political factors which sustained Junior Village.

Then FLOC's efforts were enlarged by another mission group, the Restoration Corps. They had been painting and redecorating the homes and apartments of Washington slum dwellers—absolutely free. Now, the two groups pooled resources and bought and renovated homes for Junior Village families. The Restoration Corps found their lives divided into the periods "before" and "after" they got their first family. Miss O'Connor wrote, "When you got close to that group, it was like touching the Church in Acts. Something shiny and wonderful had happened to them." [9]

By late 1969, FLOC was operating nine group foster homes. The first such home helped teenage girls from Junior Village prepare for life in a normal community; others include interracial homes in suburban areas of Arlington and McLean, Virginia. The houseparents in FLOC's first infant home are a young woman in her thirties and a grandmother of seventy, who care for four babies under six months who already showed the effects of emotional deprivation. The housemothers have reversed the traditional role in which black "mammies" cared for white children. FLOC's 1969-70 budget is $140,000, including $80,000 from the D.C. Department of Public Welfare for providing twenty-four hour care for more than forty children. [10]

For anyone wondering what the Church of the Saviour plans to do next, the answer is that they are founding a college. An international, four-year liberal arts college named for Dag Hammarskjold, the late secretary general of the United Nations, expects to enroll its first students in 1970. Land for the campus at Columbia, Maryland (a new town midway between Washington and Baltimore), is being purchased from the Rouse Corporation, developers of the new community. James Rouse, who is head of the corporation, is a member of the Church of the Saviour.

With a campaign in progress to raise six million dollars for initial construction and administrative costs, plans call for enlisting 60 percent of the faculty and student body from other countries. The polycultural college hopes to have an enrollment of 1,440 by 1980.

Dr. Robert L. McCan, the president of the college and its chief organizer, said three fundamental principles would be the institution's guidelines: "They are that we live in a global village, that reason requires that we learn to deal more effectively with rapid cultural changes, and that higher education can be made more relevant to our world situation." [11] Toward that goal "at least one-third of the student body will spend the middle two years traveling and engaging in 'practical work experience' in preparation for a vocation." He concluded the college would be "on the creative frontier but not so far out as to be lost in the wilderness." [12]

Obviously, it is easier to focus one's energies on mission to the world in a new structure like the Church of the Saviour than to try to accomplish the same ends within a more traditional congregation. Even so, where Christians are willing to open themselves to God's leading, great strides are possible in church renewal.

As they follow in the footsteps of One who took the shape of a servant, members of the Church of the Saviour have taken a towel and a basin and learned what it means to be a servant people, for the sake of Christ and the world.

NOTES

[1] Elizabeth O'Connor, *Call to Commitment* (New York: Harper & Row, Publishers, Inc., 1963), p. 34.

[2] *Ibid.*, p. 23.

[3] Elizabeth O'Connor, *Journey Inward, Journey Outward* (New York: Harper & Row, Publishers, Inc., 1968), p. 102.

[4] O'Connor, *Call to Commitment*, p. 128.

[5] *Ibid.*, p. xi.

[6] O'Connor, *Journey Inward, Journey Outward*, pp. 30-31.

[7] John D. Perry, Jr., *The Coffee House Ministry* (Richmond: John Knox Press, 1966), p. 19.

[8] Flier from The Potter's House, n.d.

[9] O'Connor, *Journey Inward, Journey Outward*, p. 48.

[10] *Harvest*, a newsletter of the Church of the Saviour, October, 1969, p. 5.

[11] *New York Times*, June 26, 1968.

[12] *Ibid.*

8

FIRST UNITED METHODIST
CHURCH IN GERMANTOWN, PA.

In a tree-lined section of Philadelphia, the buildings of First United Methodist Church in Germantown sprawl around the corner of Germantown Avenue and High Street.

Unlike most churches, early arrivals at services in this Germantown church ask the ushers to seat them in the first half dozen pews so that they may be close to what is happening. An attitude of anticipation among the congregation underscores an electric atmosphere between the ministers and the worshipers in the pews. Each expects the other to experience freedom and understanding and to respond accordingly.

"COME" AND "GO" STRUCTURES

Recognizing that in metropolitan Philadelphia the Sunday morning worship service by itself is no longer an adequate structure to celebrate the life and work of the covenant community, First Methodist has established both "come" and "go" structures as part of its congregational life.

The "come" structures include Christian Faith and Life seminars and *koinonia* groups for intensive Bible study and group interaction. A six-week series is held for prospective members. The ministers believe this approach falls somewhere between extending "the right hand of fellowship" on a Sunday morning and the two years of preparation required by the Church of the Saviour.

The "go" structures include the Glass Door, a coffee house and meeting place which reaches out to teenagers and street gangs; Wellsprings, an interfaith center seeking renewal in metropolitan Philadelphia and in local congregations; a mental health mission group; the business and industry task force of the Metropolitan Associates of Philadelphia (see chapter twelve); and Covenant

House, a bridge between human needs of the inner city and human resources of the rich-young-ruler suburbs. Virtually all of these programs were lay-inspired and continue to receive their major impetus from lay members.

From an analytical and statistical viewpoint, no sociologist would have predicted much hope for church renewal in Germantown. A changing neighborhood (in terms of income level, religious preference, and racial composition) was largely responsible for a drop in First Methodist's membership from 2000 in 1950 to 1150 in 1967. Even so, the remaining congregation was too large for change to be easy. For each member at the Church of the Saviour in Washington, Germantown had fifteen members who needed to be persuaded to try some new course of action.

Even the co-ministers of First Methodist, Robert Raines and Theodore Loder, are quite different in their outlook, although they share a basic theological compatibility. In his latest book, *The Secular Congregation,* Mr. Raines writes:

> Sunday after Sunday the theological viewpoints of each of us are exposed to scrutiny by the other and by the entire congregation. Neither of us can get away with anything. Both of us have constantly to rethink and rework our own thought in response to the thought of the other and the congregation.[1]

Both Mr. Raines and Mr. Loder are convinced of the advantages of having co-ministers. With this arrangement the two men share equally the responsibilities for sermons, church administration, counseling, weddings, and funerals. In a large church this plan is far more workable than having one man try to do everything. Both men also find that their ministries profit greatly from the interaction of ideas which they share with each other and with the two other ministers on the staff.

The ministers feel that people are attracted more by the humanity of Jesus than by his halo. They know that it will take years for the whole congregation to be turned inside out. In the meantime they recognize that "discernment leads to participation, and participation leads to witness." [2]

In the process, the ministers admit they have made mistakes. There was some controversy when seven members of the congregation took an active part in the morning service on Pentecost Sunday in 1965, but the rest of the congregation had not been prepared in advance for a novel form of worship where someone sitting in the pew next to them might walk to the chancel and speak of his concerns. In the fall of 1964, four controversial issues converged at once upon the congregation. One was the strong support by clergy and laymen for the Civil Rights Bill, coupled with the appearance of more Negroes in the congregation. During the election campaign, the church tried to have a nonpartisan seminar on the issues and the candidates but concluded later that the panel was fairer. The Arts Festival included a performance of Edward Albee's play, *The Zoo Story,* which some people found offensive. Finally, the committee working on the stewardship drive decided to use modern art in the finance brochure. When some recipients felt the design was grotesque, the committee learned that considerable advance interpretation was needed before attempting to communicate with an entire congregation via an unfamiliar art medium.

Nevertheless, enough of the core members of First Methodist have sensed the possibilities of church renewal so that they are clearly open to further exploration in creative worship and in mission outreach. One Sunday Mr. Raines' sermon combined comments on the need to increase pledges to the church budget by a minimum of 12 percent and his reactions to the presidential elections. The next week Mr. Loder gave a drama-sermon in the morning, and the Germantown Music Society presented Honegger's oratorio *King David* in the afternoon.

FREEDOM OF THE CO-MINISTERS

The freedom of the Germantown First Methodist pulpit is obvious to any worshiper. Sermons frequently deal with social concerns and political and community issues. In July, 1969, a situation involving the neighboring Cookman Methodist church became front-page news when eight protesting clergymen occupied the church and were arrested at the altar and held in jail overnight without bail. Feelings in the city ran high. Three days later Mr. Raines preached a forthright sermon outlining the views of the occupiers and of denominational officials and then spelling out where he felt the responsibility of Methodists lay.

The occupiers felt that since the Cookman church was located in a black neighborhood, it should serve black people. Instead, only one of its members was black, and its basketball court, Ping-

Pong tables, and nine classrooms were used only one day a week. Neighborhood children played on the streets because they could not afford to go swimming at the YMCA and found the recreation program of the Salvation Army too highly disciplined. When Cookman leaders refused on four occasions to discuss opening their facilities to the community, the black clergymen felt justified in occupying the church property.

Board members of Cookman church were backed by Methodist officials when they decided that no group of outsiders had any right to demand the use of private facilities or to occupy them if they were refused. On the eighth day of the occupation, a court injunction was served to have the protesters removed.

Bob Raines and several fellow ministers spent most of that Friday and Saturday meeting alternately with the occupiers and with Methodist executives. On Friday a white support group called People for Human Rights, carrying signs that said "Human Rights Before Property Rights" and "Forgive Us Our Trespasses," picketed Methodist headquarters. Within hours their protest was banned by a court injunction.

In his sermon on the next Sunday Mr. Raines said most Philadelphians probably agreed with Judge Robert Nix, Jr., who had declared: "Wrongs can't be righted by other wrongs." However, Mr. Raines added: "Others of us feel this was a religious protest to break little laws without harming people, in order to spotlight large injustices which do harm people. As a divine community with radical responsibilities, a church has something more to examine than its legal rights. If the Methodist officials had reread the Sermon on the Mount this week, they would have found no ambiguity in those words!"

Feeling that the court injunctions represented "an eye for an eye," Mr. Raines believed that the church should have offered what the demonstrators really wanted from the beginning—creative dialogue about human needs. He concluded, "It's never too late to start listening, but in Philadelphia it's later than we would like to think."

The ministers' freedom is also seen in little things. When an electronic squeal interrupted the final sentence of the pastoral prayer, Mr. Loder commented after the amen that "A squeal was an interesting way to have a prayer answered." Almost nobody in Germantown First Methodist Church is surprised when prayers are answered. In *The Secular Congregation,* Mr. Raines wrote, ". . . praying for one another is not an optional luxury for a Christian community, but a desperate necessity." [3] During the hymn before the sermon, he often kneels during the final stanza. His intensity is sensed by the congregation in the very posture of the preacher at prayer.

On summer Sundays young people in the congregation take part in the service. As the pastoral prayer, one college student described with simplicity and empathy his feelings about a society where he returned to his milk truck to find a first-grade girl eating his sandwich because she never got enough to eat at home. After that he often brought an extra sandwich and bottle of soda so that they could have lunch together. When Mr. Raines began his sermon that day, he said, "The sermon has already been preached this morning, more eloquently than I could do, out of the mouths of the young."

PREACHING WITH QUIET PASSION

The co-ministers make legitimate use of emotion in their sermons. Without becoming sentimental or theatrical, they choose fresh and vivid illustrations from history, fiction, drama, or contemporary situations. Using glimpses of people's lives helps listeners to increase their understanding of themselves and their fellow human beings.

In a sermon on "Loyalty and Sacrifice," Bob Raines quoted from emotion-packed scenes in Edward Albee's play *Who's Afraid of Virginia Woolf?* and from William Saroyan's *The Human Comedy.* In the latter, a young Western Union messenger delivers a telegram from the War Department, but the Mexican mother cannot believe her son has been killed. When the messenger gets home, he finds his mother waiting in the parlor and tells her, "I never saw anybody heartbroken that way before." [4] Mr. Raines went on to speak of the loneliness of waiting in the parlor, the kitchen, or the bedroom, yet understanding when no one comes to talk. He concluded with a paraphrase of Saroyan's words, "Sometimes your heart is too full for your tongue to speak."

One Sunday Ted Loder defined love as "what you go through with someone." In another sermon he referred to a pointed exchange between Joan of Arc and Charles Dauphin in Shaw's play *St. Joan.* Joan says pertly to the would-be king: "I tell thee it is

God's business we are here to do: not our own." [5] Mr. Loder summed up his vision of the church in these words: "It's full of lovers and laughers, of forgivers and givers, of risk takers and reconcilers, of people rolling up their sleeves and opening up their doors yet wider to the whole human family, people of all ages and races—people marching together with banners flying and voices singing to meet one revolution with a yet greater one, the revolution begun by Jesus Christ, who showed us what God's business is that we are here to do."

NOTES

[1] Robert A. Raines, *The Secular Congregation* (New York: Harper & Row, Publishers, Inc., 1968), p. 13.

[2] *Ibid.,* p. 58.

[3] Raines, *ibid.,* p. 76.

[4] William Saroyan, *The Human Comedy* (New York: Harcourt, Brace & World, Inc., 1943), p. 33.

[5] George Bernard Shaw, *St. Joan,* act 1, sc. 2 (New York: Random House, Inc., 1952), p. 89.

Issue-Shaped Ministries

9

POLITICS AND PROTEST

Issues can cause strong differences of opinion within the Christian church, but the price of serenity on Sunday may have soared too high. If today's churches ignore the crucial issues of peace, justice, and human rights—as they ignored the saturation bombing of Dresden and Hiroshima, the scandal of price-fixing in Pittsfield, and the struggle for integration in Little Rock—the whole world may walk out on the church. Surely this is too high a price to pay for serenity on Sunday!

The late Dag Hammarskjold wrote: ". . . the road to holiness necessarily passes through the world of action." [1] All seven of the case studies in the previous chapters indicate that churches involved in renewal can find ways to balance mission inside the church and mission outside the church. The commandment to love God is inextricably linked with the commandment to love one's fellowman. In modern terms, that means not only helping the man beaten on the road to Samaria but also changing the laws and power structures to make the road safe for other travelers!

Groups of Quakers have practiced direct action for over a century since they set up the Underground Railroad to help slaves flee the South. Recently they incurred government wrath by sailing the *Phoenix* to North Vietnam, loaded with ten thousand dollars' worth of medical supplies. They acted in the Quaker conviction that it is always right to show a loving concern for one's fellowman. Charged with comforting the enemy, they replied that they are comforting as best they can the victims of the enemy. To them, war is the enemy. Any war. [2]

In the parish church of Williamsburg, Virginia, the Episcopal rector felt that he could not ignore the opportunity to call for a logical explanation of America's involvement in Vietnam, especially when he had America's president and his family sitting in the front pew.

A young Lutheran minister in Omaha believed it was imperative in developing Christian fellowship to exchange social visits between young couples in his church and their counterparts in black churches. His simple suggestion caused soul-searching of the deepest order and the acute pain of transition from the status quo to the new order. Many seemed to fear these visits would lead to integration of the act of worship. The experience was captured in a vivid documentary, "A Time for Burning."

FAMILY TO FAMILY FELLOWSHIP

A similar idea had a warmer reception in Santa Barbara, California, where seventeen churches are involved in the Family to Family Fellowship.[3] The program began in September, 1965, with the combined interests of a white housewife who had joined a black church two years earlier, a businessman, and a minister of the United Church of Christ.

Two dozen families have been paired interracially and get to know each other in such social activities as potluck suppers, picnics, volleyball games, horseback riding, and walks along the beach. Once a month all the families meet together for an Evensong service, which concludes with the congregation's enthusiastic singing of the spiritual "Amen." Refreshments and a fellowship hour follow.

Like all new ideas, it has taken time to catch on. As the Negro chairman explained, "Black families have responded more slowly than whites have, partly because they suspect Whitey's motivation."

THE SERVANT CHURCH

For many churchmen, the Christ who must be preached to this century was defined by Dietrich Bonhoeffer as "the man for others." Summoned to discipleship, Christianity will be true to itself only when it exists for humanity, following the example of the Suffering Servant, who was its Lord and founder.

Servanthood calls for a new understanding of the nature of the church as a community of people, no better than anybody else, trying to be the light of the world. The church has a lot to learn from those who are open to the hurts of people. Part of its mission may well be to comfort the afflicted and afflict the comfortable.

The price tag of involvement may be high, but standing aloof in judgment costs even more. In a *Newsweek* cover story, Presbyterian theologian Robert McAfee Brown said, "In the past, controversial ministers were burned. Now they just get fired." [4] In the film *Beggar at the Gates,* Dr. Brown says, "The church is to be that group of God's people who minister to those in need. Receiving bread at the Lord's table is a phony act, unless you are concerned that all men receive bread at other tables."

THE FREEDOM MOVEMENT AND BLACK POWER

In the first decade of the civil rights movement, a few dozen stalwarts put their lives on the line in the Montgomery bus boycott, the student sit-ins, and the freedom rides. Then it became the thing for clergymen to march on Washington, to test unjust laws by nonviolent demonstrations, and to follow Martin Luther King, Jr., from Selma to Montgomery.

Drastic changes in attitudes followed the serious riots in Watts, Newark, Detroit, and two hundred other American cities. The cry of the American Negro had shifted from "freedom" to "power." The Kerner report emphasized that white racism caused the division of America into two societies—one white, one black, separate and unequal. In spite of such a need for reconciliation a Gallup poll in 1968 showed that 52 percent of the church members interviewed wanted the churches to be silent on political and social issues.

As the action of the militants has been stepped up, the church has moved back. However, the militants did not create the situation in the cities. The cities created the militants when the city fathers' lack of concern clearly proclaimed that they did not care about the problems of the have-nots, whether they are black Americans, Spanish-speaking or Indian Americans, or white Americans on welfare.

Carl McCall, a young black clergyman in the United Church of Christ, has experienced this lack of concern as an executive for the Board of Homeland Ministries and as Mayor John Lindsay's deputy administrator for human resources, dealing with a budget of two billion dollars. During the Harlem riots in 1964, Mr. McCall went to Harlem describing promises which church leaders had made to him. The church leaders didn't follow through. Now groups of the Black Panthers are winning wide support in Harlem with food programs, action projects, and promises of more to come.

In the keynote address at Andover Newton's Conference on the Ministry in 1969, Mr. McCall said: "If you would rather deal with me than the Black Panthers, you have to give me some resources to take to Harlem. I've been there before with promises I couldn't carry out. I can't go back with empty dreams."

He also explained, "Demonstration projects aren't enough of an answer. We have to make major structural changes in society. The street academies are great but they only help two hundred drop-outs. In the meantime the public school programs in New York City are crippling a million kids. *That's* the ballgame!" [5]

The Hebrew prophets would have agreed on the need for action. So do most of today's clergymen and authors. Alan Paton of South Africa writes:

> I have no higher vision of the Church than as the Servant of the World, not withdrawn but participating, not embattled but battling, not condemning but healing the wounds of the hurt and the lost and the lonely, not preoccupied with its survival or its observances or its articles, but with the needs of mankind. [6]

Today's pattern for action is for church organizations to weld together coalitions of public and private support where major decisions are made on an interracial and interfaith basis. This approach can be seen in the national Urban Coalition headed by John Gardner; in the Bedford-Stuyvesant Restoration Corps in Brooklyn; in the multimillion-dollar Operation Connection launched by the presiding bishop of the Episcopal Church; and in the Urban Training Center's "Committee for One Society." Each of these coalitions is not merely a letterhead affair but an actual partnership of blacks and whites working together for the common goals of humanity.

What of the local church, where a concerned minister knows in the loneliness of his study that the church must win back its right to be heard, even if it costs him his job? He knows that his responsibilities as a clergyman-citizen have shifted from giving the invocation at civic functions to mediating between the dispossessed and the civic power structure. He feels compelled to take *some* action, even though he feels as if he is armed with an icepick and facing an iceberg. As he struggles to find the right words and the right actions, he may remember the familiar words of British statesman Edmund Burke: "All that is necessary for the forces of evil to win in the world is for enough good men to do nothing."

The coalition or cluster idea also works in the local community. The *New York Times* estimated at least one hundred clusters of churches were functioning across the nation by late 1968. Five were related to the Portland, Oregon, Council of Churches, including one that sponsored a shopping-center ministry. On Chicago's South Side, six Protestant and two Roman Catholic churches formed the Christian Action Ministry to operate an employment center, to provide legal aid, and to offer other forms of assistance for ghetto residents.[7]

For churches that want to move into community action, one minister listed seven pointers:

> Study the church and the city; educate people about the needs that are found; select strategic problems to start with; try to relate to the local power structure; don't parallel existing programs or organizations with church-run operations, because such duplication is a waste of effort and money which would be better spent on strengthening what is already going; try to be a catalyst in the community as well as a programmer; and, finally, stress person-to-person relationships.[8]

In the beginning, one may be unrealistic to expect to involve a large proportion of the congregation. Many ministers have adopted the task force idea which enables them to blow the bugle to sign up the eager ones without exposing the rest of the congregation to judgment. After the program passes the experimental stage, a larger group can be enlisted where the need is evident for the program to continue.

INVOLVEMENT IN PRIDE'S CORNER, MAINE

Five miles from Portland, Pride's Corner, Maine, is too small to appear on many maps. Its people are rock-ribbed New Englanders, but in the last fifteen years members of the Congregational church have become involved in the world—really involved. They not only read or study about a problem or write a check or a letter, but they also reinforce "walking with their fingers" with shoe-leather involvement.

The catalyst in that situation was a new minister, Paul H. Burditt, who came in 1954 as an Andover Newton intern and decided to stay. Once the people came to trust him and accept him as their pastor, they were willing to take a serious look at his suggestions, even if they contrasted strongly with the way they had always done things.

People in Maine were not used to hearing Simon and Garfunkel music for organ preludes and special services. The minister persuaded them that for senior highs, " 'Rock of Ages' wasn't their bag."

Many of this minister's Sunday sermons are biblical; others challenge the congregation to think about problems they won't find in the Bible—the population explosion, genetic engineering, ecology, transplants, or space exploration.

In an address the pastor commented, "It's a very unnerving experience to see people taking notes on the sermon. They use them in the talk-back we have afterwards in the church parlor. When lay people react, it gives the minister a second chance to explain what he really meant. Sometimes the atmosphere gets mighty warm!" [9]

There's a conviction in Pride's Corner that "people suffer behind closed doors and somebody has to help them." They have developed a program of practical Christianity that includes a watch for moving vans—coming or going. When a woman breaks her leg while she's hanging out her wash, a procession of people appears to cook meals, to house clean, and to do the laundry until she's on her feet again. The minister added, "We try to be responsible for everyone in the community, church members or not." [10]

Twice a year Pride's Corner has an international student weekend. A caravan of cars makes a five-hour round trip to Cambridge to collect the participants, many of them post-Ph.D.'s at M.I.T. or Harvard. Paul Burditt confessed: "As we talk with them, we often feel like absolute idiots. Not only are they specialists in their fields, but as world-citizens they also are fluent in four or five languages. Most of us speak English, period. However, we take them to see the papermill, and then we picnic on the rockbound coast of Maine. We find out Moslems don't have horns, and they find out we don't have wings or even stubs. When we invited two Soviets, the FBI arrived two days before they did but we still get Christmas cards from Moscow." [11]

The church's philosophy is a simple one—to take bite-size pieces rather than try to swallow a whole loaf at once. Instead of facing all the issues of foreign policy, they invite overseas students for a weekend. Rather than trying to change Maine's entire health and education program, they regularly give volunteer time to retarded children in one institution and to mental patients in another. They don't expect to change the world, but they know Pride's Corner has become a different place.

Paul Burditt credits most of the change to the results of small groups. He said: "Jesus chose twelve because it works. Small groups work. You have to *have* the troops before you can *lead* the troops. We put on steak suppers and bean suppers and pancake suppers to attract more members and help the ones we already had get better acquainted. The week we had coffee hours on the church building plans, I put on eight pounds—but everyone had a chance to have his say. We had work nights for eighteen months and saved $30,000 in building costs. Even more important, we built a community as well as a church." [12]

The Maine Conference of the United Church of Christ has a lovely lodge on Sego Lake, forty-five minutes away. The church at Pride's Corner uses it often for retreats for the trustees or the deacons, for senior highs, couples, or any other group. To try to keep the church relevant, the members have a thorough evaluation of the entire program every five years. Ladies who have the largest living rooms are chosen as hostesses, and two promises are made to everyone who comes: What they say will be written down (but without names), and the minister won't be there. One time they ended up with eighteen pages of single-spaced comments. Twenty-three people on the church board spent a weekend at the lake considering the ideas and often reacted with "Why didn't we think of that long ago?" Some things were soft-pedaled and others spotlighted. The experience demonstrated the miracle of dialogue. Paul Burditt concluded, "I can hardly wait until tomorrow and next month, to find out what will happen to the church."

CENTRAL BAPTIST IN WAYNE, PENNSYLVANIA

When ministers act as change-agents and when lay people become deeply involved in making the church relevant in the world, exciting and sometimes controversial things begin to happen.

Twelve months before economic demands were articulated in James Forman's Black Manifesto, the assassination of Dr. Martin Luther King, Jr., became the catalyst for an unprecedented action by the Central Baptist Church of Wayne on Philadelphia's Main Line. Facing its responsibility for its black brothers, this 425-

member congregation voted to secure a $100,000 mortgage on the church property to underwrite a Martin Luther King, Jr., Memorial Fund.

Nobody quite expected the reactions that followed. Headlines and television stories appeared across the nation. A handful of members who did not feel that a mortgage was the way to advance the cause of human rights ceased active participation. Ninety new members joined the church in 1968, the largest number in Central's seventy-five year history. Most of them said they heard about the church through the King Fund. Even more significant are the vital relationships which have emerged with black leaders in Philadelphia projects assisted by the fund.

Recognizing the grave domestic crisis and the growing separation between blacks and whites, Central members agreed to "create a more just and humane society by providing financial support for programs dealing with inadequate housing, education, and employment in the Philadelphia area." After four hours of debate, the members voted 127 to 43 to establish the fund, administered by a ten-member board of trustees.

Grants are made in much the same way as foundation grants. Applications are received and investigated by the trustees. The grants themselves require a two-thirds vote by the church members. All twelve projects selected are directed by groups other than Central Baptist Church itself.

Because the congregation had just pledged $69,000 to the denomination's World Mission Campaign, no financial drive was conducted for the King Fund. When the needs became known, members and interested friends contributed $30,000 as an immediate response. The balance came from a bank loan, to be repaid through increased gifts to the church budget over a ten-year period.

The grants made are as diverse as hiring neighborhood youth to staff a summer project in North Philadelphia; supporting job-recruitment services of the Crime Prevention Association, Fellowship House in Media, and an electronics training program of Leon Sullivan's O.I.C.; equipping Gate Library in Ardmore to supplement studies in black history; matching gifts for scholarships for nine girls from low-income families at Ellen Cushing Junior College in Bryn Mawr and for college graduates at the King School for Social Change in Chester; rehabilitating a building for community planners in West Philadelphia; funding a community organizer to aid welfare persons; purchasing sewing machines for an Afro-American clothing factory in Camden; and buying land for low-cost housing and launching a day-care center in Ludlow (a ghetto-area in Philadelphia).

Obviously, the decision to take out the loan for the King Fund did not just waft in out of the blue. Some of the history of this decision dates back to 1957 when Richard L. Keach became the pastor. For years this church, like its sister churches, had assumed that changing individuals was *the* way to change society. Gradually the formation of small groups, books by Cox and Bonhoeffer, sermons and articles on renewal, and conferences on awakening the church to its mission began to have an influence. Dick Keach explained, "People found that in ministering they were ministered unto, in loving others they were loved, in risking they were strengthened, and in getting outside the box called the church they became free and involved."

Over the years the church started an integrated nursery school; resettled five Cuban families and one from Spain; sponsored a high school student from overseas through International Christian Youth Exchange each year since 1961; initiated a program with teenage gangs; and had dialogues with the deacons of a nearby black church, which resulted in forming the Main Line Community Association.

A major project on low-income housing began in 1964 with the concerns of an adult class. They hired a student researcher to live in Ludlow for a summer. Through this encounter the church joined the Ludlow Civic Association in successfully pressuring Philadelphia officials to double the number of houses rehabilitated through the city's "used house program." Housing experts consider this a better option in many neighborhoods than the usual urban renewal approach of clearing space for high-rise projects.

In a mimeographed brochure for prospective members, Mr. Keach wrote:

> Instead of a refuge from the world, now we see the church as a gathering and a scattering. We gather to hear what God would have us do, and we scatter to do it. The church becomes a launching pad to get the Christian into orbit in his real world. Religion has become less important than Christianity. Religion is doing ritual, and Christianity is picking up a cross and taking it into all of life.

All our hang-ups show and all our fears come out. All the old things we had nailed down come loose. The crucial question becomes, How do I become free to be an involved follower of Jesus Christ? What does God want of me in all this? And do I want to risk that much?

In theological terms, the members of Wayne Central believe that the Incarnation and the Resurrection are the two key doctrines. When the living Christ becomes incarnated in a person, that person burns hot and glows red. He becomes free to be the man for others. The concept of the Resurrection helps a person be raised up from old hurts and dead dogmas to move out in ministry to those places where God is calling him to be.

NOTES

[1] Dag Hammarskjöld, *Markings,* trans., Leif Sjöberg and W. H. Auden (New York: Alfred A. Knopf, Inc., 1964), p. 122.

[2] John Keats, "There Is Something Called Quaker Power," *New York Times Magazine,* March 24, 1968, p. 70.

[3] This Fellowship was described by a CBS telecast of "Lamp Unto My Feet," February 9, 1969.

[4] *Newsweek,* January 3, 1966, p. 35.

[5] From an address by H. Carl McCall at the Conference on the Ministry, Andover Newton Theological School, Newton Center, Mass., February 21, 1969.

[6] Alan Paton, *Instrument of Thy Peace* (New York: The Seabury Press, Inc., 1968), p. 69.

[7] Edward B. Fiske, "Social Action for the Parish," *New York Times,* October 13, 1968.

[8] Grace Ann Goodman, *Rocking the Ark* (New York: Board of National Missions, United Presbyterian Church in the U.S.A., 1968), p. 100.

[9] From an address by Paul H. Burditt at the Conference on the Ministry at Andover Newton, February 22, 1969.

[10] *Ibid.*

[11] *Ibid.*

[12] *Ibid.*

10

BLACK IS BEAUTIFUL

"Don't buy where you can't work." In three years that simple slogan changed the hiring patterns of twenty-nine major firms in Philadelphia without a single strike or picket sign.

The selective patronage program was organized by Dr. Leon H. Sullivan, minister of Zion Baptist Church, the city's largest Protestant congregation. He had firm support from his four hundred fellow black clergymen and their half million church members. They knew that in 1958 one-fourth of Philadelphia's population was black but "less than one percent of the sensitive, clerical, and 'public-contact' jobs were held by black people." [1] Even so, their collective purchasing power exceeded half a billion dollars a year. Dr. Sullivan added, "Even General Motors could not stand much of that." [2]

At a time when dime stores in the South were refusing to serve Negroes at lunch counters, Dr. Sullivan organized a picket line at one of the chain's stores near his church. He wrote in his book about his wife's influence in initiating the move:

> It was then that Grace asked me why I was picketing to help people eat at a lunch counter in Georgia when colored people in Philadelphia couldn't even be salesmen on bakery trucks or on soft drink trucks. It was all right, she told me, to help colored people in Alabama and Georgia, but, she said, "If you really want to do something worth while, help your people right here at home. Get them jobs. Then you will be doing something!" [3]

Her words kept ideas churning in his mind most of the night. He planned and talked to people all week and on Sunday morning launched the selective patronage program from the pulpit of Zion Baptist Church. After the service Mrs. Sullivan told him, "Well, here we go again!" [4]

The program was deceptively simple. A "priority group" of denominational leaders and key pastors met to select the company which would be the focus of attention and to choose a spokesman for that campaign. Then all four hundred ministers were invited to a church for a general gathering. Often such meetings were held at midnight to avoid schedule conflicts.

If the larger group concurred, the spokesman was joined by four other ministers in visiting the company. The top executive was asked for a record of the number of blacks employed and the positions they held, a list of the varieties of jobs the company provided, and a salary schedule. If he refused, he was told that minimum requests would be based on the sketchy information available from other employees.

After the four hundred met again, the minimum request was adopted and a deadline set, usually four to six weeks later. If the request was not met, the four hundred pastors were notified by telephone chain or by postcard and they went into their pulpits the following Sunday morning to invoke selective patronage against that company. The minimum requests were not intended as quotas but had the goal of breaking the company's entire pattern of discriminatory employment practices.

The style of the organization and the rotating chairmanships meant that anyone bent on silencing the request had to exert pressure on four hundred clergymen, not just one or two.

The same day the company complied, the priority group heard the visitation team's report and within forty-eight hours called together all four hundred ministers. If they were convinced that hiring policies had been permanently changed, they would tell their congregations; within five days 90 percent of the former patrons were buying from the company again. Directives to buy or not to buy were communicated rapidly through the churches without a single radio, television, or newspaper story! The immediate result was to open two thousand skilled jobs to black workers, plus thousands of others who were employed as an indirect effect when companies tried to head off a "visitation" to *their* president.

Each meeting with executives began and ended with prayer. The second prayer was often said outside the executive's office, because usually "he was so hot by the time the meeting was over that he did not want to hear any preachers praying about anything." [5]

The first campaign took the longest, when Tasty Baking Company was not convinced for three months that these black preachers meant business. After weeks of continuing reminders, some parishoners told their pastors that they wanted to hear about Jesus and not about Tastykake. But the clergymen persisted and eventually won their case. It proved effectively what Leon Sullivan had been saying all along: "In order to hit prejudice where it hurts most, hit it in the pocketbook!" [6]

OPPORTUNITIES INDUSTRIALIZATION CENTER

Finding that two thousand skilled jobs were available to blacks quickly created another problem. Until then there had been no need to train black men for jobs they could not have, but now there weren't enough qualified candidates to go around.

In January, 1964, Dr. Sullivan and members of Zion Baptist Church established the first Opportunities Industrialization Center (OIC) in an abandoned jail. The idea caught on like wildfire, and within three years seventy similar centers were set up across the country. They enroll twenty thousand students and have a waiting list of ten thousand more.

OIC is one of the few projects which actually reaches the hardcore unemployed with jobs and hope! Its Feeder Program teaches the 3R's, along with black history, good grooming, and what to do on a job interview. Students also learn to regard themselves as a somebody, not a nobody. Dr. Sullivan says, "I tell 'em that it's not a balloon's color that determines how high it flies, it's what is inside." [7] Next they learn technical skills, using the latest typewriters, sewing machines, lathes, chemical laboratories, computers, and other equipment donated by major industries.

The original seed money came from Zion Church, Philadelphia businesses, private contributions, and a mortgage on the Sullivan home. In the first five years, OIC placed six thousand people in 880 Philadelphia companies. These employees now earn twenty million dollars a year although 97 percent had been living below the poverty line.

Nationally, OIC itself employs three thousand people full time or part time. The combined annual budget is twenty million dollars. Ninety percent comes from government sources, and 10 percent comes from individuals, foundations, and industries. Dr. Sullivan is proud that an OIC student can be trained for an average of $1,000, while the federal job-training program costs $3,600 per student.

Problems occur—some of them serious. One OIC worker admits, "In the beginning, we were so eager to teach them typing that we neglected spelling, but we have learned from our mistakes."

"Integration without preparation is frustration." [8] One of Dr. Sullivan's favorite sayings, this statement capsulizes the purpose of OIC. The slogan for the center is "We help ourselves," and the symbol is a skeleton key that unlocks any door. Its founder emphasizes that the goal is not to give a man a diploma but to get him a good job. "A man can't eat a diploma, but he can eat and feed his family with what he can buy from a good paycheck," he adds.[9] He would like to see OIC's multiply like supermarkets in ghetto neighborhoods.

Says Edward Young, an intense young Negro who took a leave of absence from Philadelphia's IBM agency to work as Dr. Sullivan's administrative assistant, "I have seen human beings transformed here. That may sound crazy, but it's true. Leon has the knack. He can take a dispirited, hopeless individual off the street corner and in a few months turn him into a man who can look you in the eye with pride in himself. If I didn't know better, I'd call it magic." [10]

A number of experts equate what Leon Sullivan has done in the job-training field with what Martin Luther King, Jr., did for civil rights. For some Philadelphia visitors, Dr. Sullivan and his OIC headquarters almost rival the Liberty Bell and Ben Franklin's spectacles. Presidents, governors, senators, and mayors sing his praises, and his office walls are covered with plaques honoring his achievements.

In 1967 the executive director of the Philadelphia Chamber of Commerce said: "Ten years ago we were sorry that Leon Sullivan ever left the hills of West Virginia and we wished he would go back. [Then he developed the OIC program] and last year the Chamber gave Mr. Sullivan its annual William Penn award for 'business excellence!' " [11] Later he received a gold medal and ten thousand dollars from the city of Philadelphia.

MINISTER TO CHURCH AND WORLD

Dr. Sullivan's impressive six-foot-five frame is packed with boundless energy. Born in a Charleston slum, he worked his way through West Virginia State University and New York's Union Theological Seminary. After serving as an associate at Adam Clayton Powell's church in Harlem, he held a five-year pastorate in South Orange, New Jersey. When he was called to Zion church in 1950, the congregation had six hundred members. Today it has five thousand.

When Zion members resolved to tackle some urgent problems of the City of Brotherly Love, they developed a day care center; established a retirement home highly regarded by state authorities; and broke ground for Zion Gardens, a million-dollar garden apartment complex, and for the Progress Plaza shopping center. Many church members and others contribute ten dollars a month to an investment program that has provided seed money for the first black-owned aerospace industry, a garment factory, and a scholarship program.

Dr. Sullivan is emphatic on one point:

> Everything I do, I do as an outreach of my ministry. The work in which I am engaged can be understood only in that kind of context. I believe God wants me to help men to live better on earth. I believe not only in milk and honey in heaven but in ham and eggs on earth besides.[12]

> The 10-36 Plan, the Selective Patronage Program and the Opportunities Industrialization Center Program are essentially the work of the Christian Church. They represent for me the translation of my ministry into concrete, living terms. . . . With God's help, we are going to change the cries in our streets from "Burn, baby, burn" to "Build, brother, build!"[13]

NOTES

[1] Leon H. Sullivan, *Build Brother Build* (Philadelphia: Macrae Smith Co., 1969), p. 67. Used by permission.

[2] *Ibid.,* p. 81.

[3] *Ibid.,* p. 68.

[4] *Ibid.,* p. 69.

[5] *Ibid.,* p. 77.

[6] *Ibid.,* p. 79.

[7] Hans Knight, "Burn, Baby, Burn or Build, Brother, Build?" *Impact,* February, 1968, p. 6.

[8] *Ibid.,* p. 13.

[9] Sullivan, *op. cit.,* p. 124.

[10] *Impact,* February, 1968, p. 6.

[11] *New York Times,* November 7, 1967.

[12] Sullivan, *op. cit.,* p. 21.

[13] *Ibid.,* pp. 176, 179.

Ecumenical Ministries

11

CLUSTER MINISTRIES IN METROPOLIS

Not only have some local churches found innovative ways to minister to the needs of contemporary man, but other churches have found ways to join together in various forms of an ecumenical ministry with a zest previous generations would have thought impossible. These cluster ministries have been made possible by the new atmosphere of openness between churches of different traditions; and they have been made necessary because of the tremendous needs which dwarf the efforts of any individual church.

ECUMENICITY IN KANSAS CITY

The ringing of a 75-pound bronze bell in downtown Kansas City may eventually have reverberations reminiscent of the sound of Martin Luther's hammering his ninety-five theses on the chapel door in Wittenberg, Germany. This bell was first rung by Pope John XXIII to open the Second Vatican Council in Rome, and then it was presented by its makers to St. Mark's Church in Kansas City, the nation's first joint Protestant-Roman Catholic congregation. The new venture hopes to bridge chasms between Protestant and Catholic, black and white, affluent and disadvantaged. Except for separate Sunday worship services for Catholics and Protestants, all functions of the new church are unified.

In every sense a ministry in metropolis, St. Mark's brings Christian unity out of the visionary sphere of upper echelon conferences and enlists it in a specific, local congregation. Supported equally by Roman Catholics, Presbyterians, Episcopalians, and the United Church of Christ, the church is housed in a contemporary structure of sandblasted concrete and steel, costing four hundred thousand dollars. Dedicated in November, 1968, a semicircular sanctuary seats three hundred persons. Worshipers face a single liturgical center, which maintains the distinctiveness and integrity of each communion's heritage. Bright-colored banners, made by a group of nuns, drape the walls between the twelve tall pillars. The building provides an esthetic center related to black culture that an inner-city neighborhood proudly calls its own. A 25-foot roughhewn cross is as realistic as the community it faces. In six square blocks fifteen thousand people, mostly blacks, live in crowded high-rise apartments in the architectural style sometimes known as "early urban renewal." More than half of the residents are on welfare. But St. Mark's is far more than a social service institution. It is a strong community of Christians, a vibrant demonstration of ecumenical corporateness, and a place where blacks are participants, not recipients.

What has emerged in the shape of St. Mark's is the realization of a dream envisioned a decade ago by Kenneth S. Waterman, who went to Kansas City in 1957 to develop new forms of inner-city ministry for the Presbyterian Board of National Missions. As the minister of a sagging church in the ghetto, he launched programs for teenagers and senior citizens, added Negro gospel music to the worship liturgy, and took on welfare casework. When he became acquainted with the minister of the nearby Congregational church and personnel from Catholic Charities, they worked together on certain projects.

Active planning for St. Mark's began in July, 1966, a year before Mr. Waterman joined the World Council of Churches' staff in Geneva, Switzerland. He and his Congregational colleague felt strongly that their run-down church plants and dwindling congregations should be replaced by a dynamic ecumenical enterprise with enough resources to aid the inner city. Amazingly, they convinced the bishops of the Roman Catholic and Episcopal dioceses to lend their support. Catholics and Protestants have shared worship facilities on college campuses and military bases, but St. Mark's Church was to become a "first" as a brand-new united parish that Roman Catholics and Protestants sponsored together.[1]

The team ministry at St. Mark's includes a Benedictine priest, who spent twenty-five years in the Ozarks and now heads the parish's social action program, and three Protestant ministers, who have each had inner-city experience.

To fulfill its functions of action, involvement, and service, the new church has extensive facilities for recreation, teaching, drama, a library, food service, and offices. Outside, a pleasant, railed plaza has tables for dining and dialogue. Program plans call for home care service, counseling for parolees and others, job placement, tutoring, and activities for preschool youngsters, youth, and senior citizens.

Such an advancement of Christian unity at the grass roots level required the influence of Pope John and the war on poverty, coupled with strong concern of people to give the disenfranchised a clear voice in society. In Kansas City, there are answers blowing in the wind!

THE GRASS ROOTS CHURCH

The ecumenical movement must be local if it is to be effective, urges Stephen C. Rose, Presbyterian former editor of *Renewal Magazine,* in his book *The Grass Roots Church.* He calls for cooperative ministries to serve clusters of congregations, guiding them in the functions of chaplaincy, teaching, and "abandonment." By late 1968 well over one hundred of these clusters had been established across the nation.

Under chaplaincy he includes worship, preaching, and the pastoral ministry; and under teaching, the professional instruction of the laity in year-round teaching centers. He sees both as the resources needed by the laity if they are truly to become the servant church. For him teaching is the bridge on which the Christian moves from celebration and seeking to action and involvement and back again to worship.

His concept of "abandonment" calls for coordinating church efforts in social action with secular programs and developing specialized ministries. His book sums this up in one paragraph:

> The Church that takes abandonment seriously will place emphasis on experimental ministries, on participation in direct action movements designed to bring about political, economic, and racial justice, and on the mission of the laity in the scientific laboratories, the legislative assemblies, the centers of youth culture, the schools, and the wretched compartments where the aged are prematurely buried. It will be concerned with the humanization of life where it is lived.[2]

He believes that, if they dared to do so, a group of urban churches could restructure their resources in staff and lay leadership, buildings, and finances to bring about a cooperative ministry serving the entire neighborhood. Those who wanted to preach would preach, those who chose to counsel would counsel, those who preferred to teach would teach—rather than each one attempting the futile goal of becoming the "everything" minister. The time and money saved by avoiding duplicate services could be used to develop creative new ministries.

Although it is unquestionably true that the church in action would attract more followers than the church in repose, several serious problems must be resolved if Mr. Rose's proposal is to be practiced. Greatly increased relevancy is not necessarily assured simply by moving the locus of power from denominational headquarters to the grass roots. For example, he is undoubtedly right that there is no need to have a dozen denominations preparing separate sets of curriculum materials, but his assumption seems to be that amateurs at the grass roots can prepare more effective teaching materials than a presumably expert staff of writers and editors in New York, Philadelphia, St. Louis, or some other center. He also seems to take too lightly such problems as the genuine guidance given by denominations to local churches, the role of theological seminaries, the importance of fund-raising programs, and the massive tasks involved in retraining leaders for radically revised forms of church life.

Significant as these as-yet-unsolved problems may be, Mr. Rose seems on the track of an extremely compelling idea. Such clusters have been tried to various degrees in Kansas City, Rochester, Minneapolis, and a hundred other cities. They may well be the key to a sweeping kind of church renewal that would revolutionize Christian life and mission for generations to come.

NEIGHBORHOOD ECUMENICAL MINISTRIES IN ROCHESTER

The biblical concept of the covenant relationship has been paramount in the rediscovery of community in the church and in the neighborhood. Having decided to remain in the inner city, the Lake Avenue Baptist Church of Rochester, New York, is experiencing a renewal within its own membership, despite strong tensions on certain issues, and is committed to a pacesetting program in grass roots ecumenism which involves joint planning, funding, and staffing by sixteen Protestant and Roman Catholic churches in the northwest sector of Rochester.

Dr. William R. Nelson, who was deeply involved in the new

emphasis after he joined the team ministry in 1965, gives a capsule definition of the churchmen's motivation: "Theology only has meaning if it has something to say both to the church and to the world." [8] He served in a cooperative three-way arrangement as the teaching minister on the staff of Lake Avenue Baptist Church, as a missionary appointee of the American Baptist Home Mission Societies, and as a lecturer in field education on the faculty of Colgate Rochester Divinity School/Bexley Hall.

Lake Avenue's deep involvement in its immediate neighborhood emerged gradually during the course of the last ten years. In 1963, when the congregation decided to remain near downtown Rochester, it recognized that church renewal required more than new paint, plumbing, and plaster, or even a new order of worship. For seven years two student ministers had conducted programs, largely recreational, for neighborhood children. Then came the riots in the black community of Rochester in the summer of 1964. The Rochester Area Council of Churches, through its participating denominations, responded to the challenge by funding a broad-based community organization. The pressure tactics which followed were aimed primarily at securing wider employment opportunities for black residents at Kodak, one of Rochester's major industries. The tensions mounted at Lake Avenue when its senior minister, Dr. George W. Hill, became the key public interpreter for FIGHT (Freedom, Integration, God, Honor—Today), a Saul Alinsky type of community organization in Rochester. Recognizing the need for social change, Dr. Hill accepted the leadership post even though he was fully aware that many of his church members were Kodak employees.

Additional conflicts were caused when the church became involved in joint programming with neighboring Roman Catholic churches to the dismay of a few strong anti-Catholics. During most of its first century of ministry, Lake Avenue had given half of its budget to underwrite mission programs around the world. Now its fourteen hundred members were being asked to deal directly with nearby people rather than just raising money so that someone else could carry on the mission. To experience a spiritual renewal to complement the building's physical renewal, the congregation was challenged to share in the outward journey of expanding its mission to the community and also to explore the inward journey of deepening their life together.

The emphasis on the inward journey began in October, 1966, with a weekend retreat led by Mark Gibbs, an articulate lay theologian from the Church of England, and was expanded in 1967 with a weekend happening directed by a visiting team of twenty-five volunteers from the Faith at Work Movement, which stresses a depth approach to dialogue through small groups. The visitors were as varied as a Ph.D. from Lehigh University and Redcap #42 from Grand Central Station.

Nearly four hundred members took part in the varied program, which was followed by special small group emphases in the School of Missions. This twin approach resulted in expanding the number of *koinonia* groups in the congregation from two to twelve, involving over one hundred persons. Two groups stressed Bible study, nine discussed current books, and one emphasized personal sharing.

After the Faith at Work weekend, one member said: "We're not the same church anymore. Something has been released in our midst that we don't understand. It gave us new hope, a new look at the gospel and showed us that Christ is at work in our lives."

THE LAITY'S ROLE

At a breakfast session during the American Baptist Convention in Pittsburgh in 1967, Ray Kicklighter, a research scientist at Kodak, described the important role played by the laymen of the church in the development of its new ministries to the community. He pointed out that the laymen were not trying to add merely another program because "like most church members, our people need one more meeting like they need a hole in the head." Rather, they were seeking answers to some of the basic questions about the church—its purpose and function in the community. Undergirding their search were basic convictions that the church could be renewed and that any effective action had to be ecumenical in its involvement of the people in the community. The congregation as a whole backed up these convictions by voting to undertake the program sixteen months before a staff person was called to lead them in the implementation of their plans.[4]

The changing neighborhood involved is in Rochester's first residential fringe, near the imposing Kodak Tower. Most of the people in this working-class community are Italian Catholics, with Spanish-speaking and Negro residents nearby. When Bill Nelson and his family moved into a residence only a block from the church, he became Lake Avenue's most visible identification with its own neighborhood. Here was a minister who could speak as a property owner and whose children attended local schools.

Since the formation of the Northwest Ecumenical Ministry in the spring of 1968, six Catholic and ten Protestant churches respond to their own constituencies in terms of their usual traditions. However, when these sixteen churches look outward to the community, they plan, finance, staff, and implement what they do as one church. This relationship is based on mutual trust among the clergy and laity. It involves common concern for the community, growing awareness of each other as persons, a sharing of ideas and feelings, cooperative planning for mission, involvement in specific programs, and continuing evaluation of effectiveness.

ECUMENICAL ALPHABET SOUP

The initials of the resulting programs sound like a cross between governmentese and a cookbook: NEM, IDEA, NIP, STIR, AYM, and WEDGE. Using the three functions of the renewed church outlined by Stephen Rose—chaplaincy, teaching, abandonment—the cooperative ministries in northwest Rochester have been described succinctly in a report prepared by the Lake Avenue church:

> 1. *Chaplaincy* refers to the role of the clergy in worship, pastoral care, and preaching. The revitalization of the "Northwest Clergy Group" [at one time called Northwest Ecumenical Ministry—NEM] was a key factor in the development of grass roots ecumenism. Mutual trust and respect at this level opened the door to many other areas of involvement. Worship has been a regular part of "Interfaith Dialogue in the Edgerton Area," [IDEA], growing out of Bible study among the laity of the "core churches." The celebration of Lent was preceded by an Ecumenical Worship Service and concluded with an Ecumenical Worship Service. . . . The combined choir from "core and fringe churches" made a lasting impression.
>
> 2. *Teaching* refers to the equipping of the laity for the communication of the Christian faith. Training a staff of forty adults and teenagers for the "Neighborhood Interchurch Program" . . . enabled the "core churches" to engage in a cooperative ministry with children for the first time. Using the method of creative drama, the program was based on the Biblical record of salvation history.[5]

After the first year, virtually all of the teaching was turned over to the high school youth as their mission in the church. By 1968

NIP involved 150 lay persons and about 500 children from eight churches in a month-long summer program which was operated in five church buildings. An ecumenical staff of forty teenagers continued this ministry with children during the school year in the Community Center at Lake Avenue. A major part of the training was in small groups called together for biblical and theological reflection on the meaning of the Christian faith.

To prepare seminarians from Colgate Rochester and St. Bernard's Seminary for the urban ministry, a program was developed in 1967-1968 called STIR or Strategy Training in Renewal. Guided by a coordinating committee of ministers and priests, it involved thirty students who learned as they participated in ecumenical group ministries. The enthusiasm of Bishop Fulton Sheen for this urban training program was a strong asset during the time he was in Rochester.

The report from the church continues by identifying *abandonment* with the participation of laymen in mission to the community without seeking to dominate or control the community. This emphasis actually came first but required the support of chaplaincy and teaching, as outlined above, to sustain the spirit of abandonment.

Thirty lay persons are discovering the meaning of abandonment in the Area Youth Ministry (AYM) with alienated senior highs. Working largely with school dropouts and other troubled youth through "The Place" at Dewey Avenue Presbyterian Church, the staff also shares in weekend retreats and street ministry. A series of biblical word studies have provided the occasion for theological reflection upon their task.

In volunteering 4000 hours of time a year, these lay persons have stood with the teenagers in many situations. They have helped them find jobs, apartments, and temporary homes. They have taught teenagers to drive, gone with them to court, and sobered them up. They have listened to their triumphs, romances, and corny jokes as well as to the deep questions they were raising about life, values, and faith. They have learned that the wilder the behavior of teenagers, the louder is their cry for help.

Other laity have chosen to relate to the structures of poverty by helping inner-city residents form a community development corporation known as WEDGE (named after an industrial symbol for change), a coalition of suburbanites and Brown Square residents.

The suburbanites come from Lake Avenue and from the Community of the Servant of God, a Roman Catholic non-territorial church. The emerging community concerns include the enforcement of housing codes; the health hazards imposed upon Brown Square through the improper operation of junk yards; zoning and land use; recreation; and education. One Brown Square mother wrote, "Now I know the church is listening and ready to help, to get dirty, to give strength, to get involved."

In Rochester, the clergy are primarily catalysts and enablers, not directors. The laity involved in each of the group ministries or action committees return to their respective congregations with new insights and vital experiences which stimulate the interest of many others. What is happening in Rochester seems a hopeful sign of new church unity which transcends the artificial barriers of religion, culture, and race.

NOTES

[1] "A Fresh Breeze Is Blowing," *United Church Herald,* October, 1968, p. 18.

[2] Stephen C. Rose, *The Grass Roots Church* (New York: Holt, Rinehart & Winston, Inc., 1966), p. 74.

[3] Harvey A. Everett, et al., "The Rochester Story," *Creative Ministry 15* (Valley Forge: American Baptist Home Mission Societies, May, 1967), p. 4.

[4] *Ibid.,* p. 3.

[5] From "Vignettes on the Quest for Renewal," a mimeographed report of the Lake Avenue Baptist Church, Rochester, N.Y., May, 1967, pp. 4-5.

12

MINISTRIES TO SECULAR STRUCTURES

"Welcome to the many exciting worlds of Boston" is a sign at Logan Airport that symbolizes the fragmentation of life. Because society today is sharply divided into so many separate worlds, some ministries can be more effective if they are geared to be an actual part of the secular structures. This has long been true for chaplains in hospitals and on university campuses. The same approach is now being explored in ministries to such structures as city government, industries, shopping centers, and regional areas.

METROPOLITAN ASSOCIATES OF PHILADELPHIA

Theologian Dietrich Bonhoeffer and editorials from today's *Wall Street Journal* are quoted with equal competence by those involved in the Metropolitan Associates of Philadelphia (MAP), an ecumenical action-research project designed to evoke and provoke the institutions of metropolis to respond effectively to involvement in social change.

Most churchmen agree that one of the basic goals of the Christian church is to put faith into action. MAP attempts to do this through a highly creative staff, structure, and program. Under the leadership of Richard Broholm, a group of twenty clergymen and 150 laymen are trying to devise a form of public ministry in the business, governmental, and social organizations of their city. Their aims are to find out what issues are critical for Philadelphia, discover how decisions are made which affect the city's life, and suggest how Christians can help institutions realize the role in society that God has given them.[1]

Even MAP's location and structure are symbolic of its ministry. Its offices are one block from City Hall and across the street from John Wanamaker, Philadelphia's largest department store. The annual budget of $125,000 is supported by American Baptists, Episcopalians, Missouri Synod Lutherans, the United Church of Christ, Methodists, and the National Council of Churches. The project was launched in 1965 under the impetus of the World Council of Churches' study on the missionary structure of the congregation, which emphasized the role of the laymen in the secular city.

To discern, participate in, and celebrate God's activity in the city, the project's founder, Dr. Jitsuo Morikawa, assembled an impressive team that combines youth, brains, and staunch commitment. The MAP staff includes an interdisciplinary team of researchers representing the fields of theology, psychology, organizational theory, and systems analysis. Others are worker-ministers, men with both theological and secular training, who hold secular jobs and meet regularly with MAP staff and lay associates. The largest group and the heart of the project are the lay associates who are already employed in widely varied positions of responsibility and who give civic leadership in many areas of Philadelphia's life. They were selected because they are theologically sensitive and deeply involved in church and world.

The MAP budget provides the salaries of the professional staff and relocation expenses and pension dues for the worker-ministers, who receive regular salaries from their secular employers, as do the lay associates.

When churchgoers express surprise that the worker-ministers are not leading local churches, they receive a wide sweep of answers. Bill Cameron, director of the Fair Housing Council of Delaware Valley, says: "The social issue in my suburban parish was race, particularly open housing, but I couldn't mobilize the church to act. I feel I'm more effective now in organizing people for this issue." [2] From the vantage point of full involvement, they seek what it means to be obedient Christians in the world of work.

The MAP action-research program revolves around several action-research task forces which represent the broad areas of life in Philadelphia. MAP's director, Richard Broholm, recognizes that rapid change is an inescapable characteristic of today's society, and traditional assumptions and ways of acting no longer seem adequate or relevant. In a report to the MAP board he wrote:

> Within the last decade there has been growing concern within the Church to see the ministry of the laity not in terms of what laymen do

within and for the Church but rather what they do within and for the secular world of work and politics. . . .

The twin concerns to understand the nature and goals of rapid change and the role of the laity in shaping this change constitute the wellsprings for the existence of Metropolitan Associates of Philadelphia. . . .

The change to which we are committed is for the sake of a more human society in which all men fully participate in the political, economic and social decisions which affect them, and in which racism and poverty are eliminated. We are concerned about the question of institutional change for the sake of the humanization of both the advantaged and disadvantaged.[3]

At one business and industry task force session, the major presentation was made by a lay associate, Robert McLean III, an industrial marketing expert. Typical of the high caliber of lay associates, he is a Yale graduate, an ex-Marine, and an active Episcopalian. In his mid-thirties, he is married and has three children. He spends about five hours a week with MAP because he believes it "is an attempt to take secular life more seriously and . . . a way to be responsible about God's action in history." [4]

Each year MAP also sponsors "issue workshops," a lecture and discussion series on crucial issues to which the public is invited. Subjects have included black power, civil disobedience, and participatory democracy.

Another major thrust of MAP has been the development of an Action-Research Strategic Planning Manual to analyze institutions and plan for change within them. Dr. Robert Hoover, chairman of the department of urban studies at the University of Cincinnati, spent 1966-1967 developing the basic research tool. He worked with a task force of six men who used a fifteen-page questionnaire to examine the attitudes toward change and the expressed or implied goals of their respective businesses, social agencies, or government offices. MAP also maintains a continuing self-study effort, which is called the "strategic planning group."

In eighteen months, MAP members made 150 presentations of their unusual program to local church groups. They also share their findings through published papers, conferences, and workshops. Measuring results of such a complex program is far from an easy task, but some things are clearly the results of MAP.

For example, MAP has the mobility to respond to a crisis situation. November 17, 1967, became known as Black Friday in Philadelphia when the police chief was heard on local radio stations ordering his men to turn police dogs loose on teenagers demonstrating at a public high school. Within forty-eight hours MAP members met with some of the students involved and helped to launch a group called People for Human Rights. A worker-minister helped organize Teachers for Social Action, a reform group within the Philadelphia Federation of Teachers. A third response was the formation of the Philadelphia Crisis Committee, which brought together newspaper executives and black militants and later organized a telephone network of sixty civic agencies and religious groups, since extended to neighborhood organizations, *ad hoc* coalitions, and other concerned groups.

Another MAP staff member was instrumental in forming the Philadelphia Council of Professional Craftsmen, which is now supported by five museums and colleges of art. This new group received the vote of a newspaper art critic as the year's "most promising art organization."

MAP staff members also responded when they learned that citizen participation in Philadelphia's poverty program was being effectively short-circuited by certain top administrators of the Mayor's Philadelphia Anti-Poverty Action Council (PAAC). A MAP worker-minister employed by PAAC tried to see if he could bring about greater citizen participation, as called for in Title II of the federal government's enabling act. He tried from the inside and was fired.

After that happened, the Maximum Participation Movement came into existence during the spring of 1966. One of the few citizens' groups of its kind in the nation, its members included neighborhood people, representatives of Community Action Councils, academic leaders, ministers, and other concerned citizens. At least in part because of the efforts of the Maximum Participation Movement (and the blunders of PAAC) "Washington has demanded the establishment of an entirely new War on Poverty structure for the city of Philadelphia." [5]

"Concern" and "involvement" are apt words to describe Metropolitan Associates. They occur often among MAP-men, who seem almost unaware that they are the church's avant-garde.

AGORA IN OAK BROOK SHOPPING CENTER

In Oak Brook, Illinois, the church is moving out from the cathedral to the people. This shopping center ministry is called

"Agora," the Greek word for marketplace. Its director is Donald Kelly, a minister without a pulpit. The headquarters for his parish of shopping center employees is a Danish modern office in the Oak Brook professional building arcade. It is a meeting place for people and ideas in an attempt to "humanize the work scene." [6]

Although Agora is sponsored by the United Church of Christ, its "ministry of listening" is open to people of all faiths—or no faith. It is something of a bridge between the underground church and the visible organized church which is more familiar to most Americans.

Don Kelly is convinced that it is important for the church to help people ask the "meaning questions." In a newsletter he wrote, "Faith and vocation must be of one piece if we are to be whole persons."

Shortly after arriving at Oak Brook in 1964, Mr. Kelly learned that he could not carry on leisure-time programs in a work world. Time pressures and sheer fatigue are basic facts of life for virtually all Oak Brook employees. Nobody needs busywork! As a result, anything Agora offers must be vitally important and of serious concern. In an interview he explained: "Many people here are in decision-making positions and bear major responsibility for shaping the possible into the real. Present indications are that we should concentrate our ministry on continuing education and opportunities for true dialogue."

Agora emphasizes depth involvement and is not overly concerned with the number of people contacted by its programming week by week. To deal with the value questions of individuals and organizational structures, it has set up a series of seminars where executives write case studies of their own business practices to help them define the roots of their decisions.

On Monday nights in the conference room of the Executive Plaza building, Don Kelly listens as these executives examine the larger questions of life. "I . . . try to understand their moral binds. I want to know what kind of criteria they use when reaching their decisions," [7] he explained.

Agora resembles conventional church programming when it does individual counseling or conducts discussion groups on plays or novels like Joseph Heller's *Catch-22*. Mr. Kelly muses: "Sometimes the easiest and best way to talk to a man is over a martini or a cup of coffee. If you hit him at just the right moment, you might learn what is really on his mind. But the trick is to accomplish this in a group session." [8]

Breakfast has been found to be a good time for more structured study groups. Also, a few times a week at noon, tables are reserved in one of the Oak Brook restaurants for depth conversations which force people to think and to interact on crucial issues.

Human relations is an area posing serious problems for many Oak Brook employees. In a form of ministry still unknown to many local churches, Agora has been conducting sensitivity training sessions. Called "marathons," they last for twenty-four to thirty-six hours over a weekend and involve ten Oak Brook center employees in nonstop discussions. The sessions are intended to help each person increase his own self-understanding and form an awareness of group functions and the psychological needs of other people.

Recognizing that he must be constantly aware of the latest discoveries and techniques applicable to the ministry, the Agora director is involved in an intensive program of continuing education. He has attended seminars at Princeton University, a month-long session of the National Training Laboratory, and shorter seminars at the Industrial Relations Center, the University of Chicago, Urban Training Center, and other locations. He also has acquired firsthand job experience by spending summer periods working at Sears and Stouffers in the Oak Brook center.

Agora is one of nearly two dozen shopping center ministries scattered across the nation. One of the most ambitious opened late in 1968 at the Landmark Center in Washington, D.C. Launched with Presbyterian initiative, it envisions a staff of six to eight and a budget of $400,000.

By operating "where the action is," Agora and its kindred programs offer a valid ministry for the businessman faced with an ethical decision, the secretary alienated from her fellow employees, or the clerk involved in cutthroat competition for sales. Such ministries are a way for the church to say, "We care and will help where we can, as you face the meaning questions of life."

BOSTON INDUSTRIAL MISSION

Since the major influence in most businessmen's lives is not their homes but their work, industrial mission begins by meeting men in the midst of their real experiences on the job—whether on the assembly line in Detroit, in the insurance vice-president's office in Newark, or in the research laboratory on Route 128, Boston's "brain highway." Nearly a dozen cities have taken a leaf from the book of the worker-priests in France, the evangelical academies in Germany, and the Sheffield Industrial Mission in England to launch industrial mission programs that extend from Wall Street to Detroit to San Juan.

The Boston Industrial Mission, called BIM for short, is centered in the burgeoning research and development industry, a field which is itself experiment-minded and future-oriented. Someone has said, "Change is that industry's business." By the very nature of things, researchers are often caught between the morality of wealth and power and the morality of human growth.

Scott Paradise, BIM's young director, said recently:

> Since its business is knowledge and its interest is in innovation, the research and development industry has a special role to play in modifying our society to enhance human growth for all. Without more knowledge about the ways to organize cities, control air and water pollution, improve education, prevent wars, and decide on the optimum population, our social advance is akin to stumbling down a toy-littered stairway in the dark.[9]

With the government as their chief customer, many executives and scientists share a sense of anxiety about the military nature of much of their work. Some are interested in discussions of ethics and decision making or in exploring the possibilities of using the systems approach to solve complex social problems. Others wonder, "On what basis do we decide whether an innovation brings dangers or social costs outweighing the social benefits?" Since the church seems to be the only institution explicitly dedicated to understanding what is good for man and enhancing these values, the church must not duck its responsibilities for the world of industry. Somehow, laymen have to be enlisted as colleagues committed to the task of theological discovery.

Scott Paradise of Boston agrees with Hugh White of Detroit and other leaders of industrial mission who feel that the proper purpose of the church in relation to society is to "influence the influencers." Among other goals of industrial mission, they recognize the importance of bringing together various levels of management and labor for critical and creative thinking about human values and social change; exploring the ethical, religious, and vocational dimensions of the meaning of life and the importance of personhood and justice; and conveying feedback to the religious institutions about the actual situation in today's urban world.

Industry's initial reaction to these men in their midst was to regard them as wild animals escaped from the zoo—probably not as dangerous as lions but at least as unusual as zebras. Most men in management positions saw no connection at all between what they heard from the pulpit on Sunday morning and the decisions they had to make on Monday morning. They could see no more reason for ministers to be concerned with how industry operated than for a company president to give advice on baptizing babies.

In Detroit, after two and a half years of humble listening to people at all levels of labor and management, the industrial mission staff finally received a green light from the president of a small company to conduct lunchtime discussion groups among his men. This free access to the plant gave them more significant contacts in a day than they could have had otherwise in a week. They discussed crucial issues with plant and personnel managers and with workers during union meetings and in informal lunch-box groups on the plant floor. They discussed several key issues, such as whether pull or skill should be the primary basis of job advancement, and the toll that job pressures and industrial mobility took upon the meaning of work and individual freedom. They sought honesty, not harmony, in their discussions.

Occasionally staff members found themselves caught in the middle. Deeply sympathetic with the civil rights movement and active participants in many of its activities, they held back when a civil rights picket line was thrown around one of the plants where they worked. They felt that to picket there, at that time, would destroy relationships that were slowly being built with the top administrators; they were expecting that these relationships would ultimately put them in a strong advisory position on civil rights and many other matters.[10]

Choices also had to be made between a ministry to the powerful and service to the powerless. Because top management understood the community service approach better, the staff was often tempted to give a disproportionate amount of time to community problems that had no relationship with industry's real problems. Nevertheless, community service to the powerless was not the main reason the Industrial Mission had been established in Detroit or Boston.

A study group in Boston soon found that the black power advocates and industrialists are engaged in two different ball games, each playing by a different set of rules. Although the gross earnings of Roxbury, the Harlem of Boston, have been estimated at eighty million dollars, nearly all of this money ends up in the suburbs, where the manufacturers, car dealers, landlords, finance company managers, and similar people live. The research and development (R&D) industries themselves are also located in suburban areas, which are hard for the ghetto dweller to reach by public transportation. To relate the R & D industry to the urban crisis, the Boston Industrial Mission set up a program to explore ways in which the corporations can respond to the immediate crisis and also to investigate how the technical skills being developed can be employed to deal with the problems of the city.

In a personal narrative on the early years of the Detroit Industrial Mission, where he served for eight years before going to Boston in 1965, Scott Paradise outlined the qualifications which he felt were necessary as a style of life for an industrial missioner. These include constant initiative, involvement, a genuine fondness for people, positive pleasure in building a network of relationships, confidence that he can contribute something worthwhile to industry, and sensitivity to positive response when a man is approached and wants to be involved on the side of justice and human growth.[11]

SAN FERNANDO VALLEY PROJECT

The nation's fastest growing city is found in the 225 square miles of the San Fernando Valley near Los Angeles. The population had already totaled over one million persons several years ago. Often called "a valley of strangers," there was ample evidence that people did not care about their neighbors. The high mobility rate of 37 percent accentuated problems like juvenile delinquency, racial discrimination, and a lack of civic pride. Rootlessness had removed the social shock absorbers so that minor family problems often became major crises. Several corporations sent people there to train for jobs in places all over the world, saying, "If they can communicate there, they can communicate anywhere." After intensive study of this living laboratory of social and cultural change, a German sociologist wrote that it was "a pure example of the emerging shape of secular societies."

In the midst of this still unformed community, which in 1962 included 800,000 people with no active church affiliation, the Lutheran Church in America launched a pilot project to develop a sense of the servant church in society, both among Lutheran congregations and toward the community as a whole. As the minister-director, the Lutherans named Clifton M. Weihe, who had spent twelve years planning and administering evangelism programs throughout North America for the Lutheran Board of Social Missions. With no precedents except some gleanings from lengthy European study trips, he was charged with coordinating sixteen parish programs in a district model that would be a workable administrative unit, expanding the horizons of each parish to include other churches and the current realities of the world, and encouraging dialogue and understanding in this valley of strangers. Where each church had been playing its own solo, he was to organize a symphony.

Role of Laymen. Quality lay leaders were a major factor in the project's effectiveness. Aided by means of retreats, a lay school of theology, and several sessions of a lay cabinet, top laymen were discovered in such varied posts as aerospace administrators at Lockheed, Douglas, and the Jet Propulsion Laboratory; professors at Valley State College and UCLA; a branch manager of the Fuller Brush Company; and a mortgage executive. Their involvement was planned to liberate the laity from the constraints of a single parish structure and to help them grow in understanding the demands of the servant community.

The most significant program was the San Fernando Valley Forum, which began with a request from Calvin H. Hamilton, director of the Los Angeles Planning Commission, to hold area-wide discussions aimed at shaping the city for human good by adding the moral and ethical dimension. The printed announcement said to the community, "You will be affected by the Valley's future, why not be involved?"

Three series of discussions were conducted, with a total of fourteen sessions. All three had excellent speakers, thoughtful discussions in small groups and plenary sessions, and an impressive attendance.

Within the Congregations. Pastoral attitudes largely determined degrees of congregational participation. Since these were "come" churches, not "come, equip, and go out" churches, major changes of outlook were needed. Mr. Weihe met with each parish evangelism committee, emphasizing their tasks of getting the gospel into the church, getting the church into the world, and getting the world into the church. In many parishes dialogue groups resulted. Such groups seem to be one of the best methods of teaching and recruiting available in today's church.

Interparish Cooperation. A primary goal of the project was to develop an area strategy for interparish cooperation. As they worked together to seek new forms of cooperative ministries, the parishes showed the Valley community that they could be partners, not competitors. A clear esprit de corps developed, and feelings diminished that a church was doing someone else's job when its members lent a brotherly hand.

The first major program, "Good Neighbor Visits," proved a breakthrough in parish evangelism efforts. Members of various congregations joined together to call on all the residents of a given neighborhood simply to encourage a spirit of goodwill. The visitors said: "We *are* your neighbors and want to be good neighbors. We hope you feel the same." They left a folder about the church and willingly answered any questions they were asked, but they made no attempts to get information for a religious census nor to conduct living room conversations about the meaning of church membership.

Even this low-key approach was received coolly at its first attempt as the visitors went out from a racially integrated church across the boulevard into a totally white section that was at least 80 percent unchurched. Succeeding Good Neighbor Visits were set up by eight parishes and involved 321 visitors. In one church the minister reported that over half of the 117 adult new members who joined that year had been identified during the Good Neighbor Visit. The project jolted congregations into doing more visiting in their own parishes.

The San Fernando Project was successful in reaching individuals. On one of the Good Neighbor Visits, a brochure was left under the door of someone who was not at home that afternoon. That act led to a series of experiences which changed that person's life. After growing up in a convent, she had become a well-known screenwriter in Hollywood. She married a man whom she loved deeply, and they became quite wealthy. During the depression, her husband died suddenly of a heart attack, and financial security vanished in a crumbling stock market. Inner depression welled up, and one night she became a would-be suicide. When she emerged from the hospital, she began going to church every Sunday, searching for peace of mind and soul.

When she found the brochure at her door, she decided to visit the neighboring Lutheran church. She told the pastor she was not a Lutheran; in fact, she was not really anything. To her surprise, he came to visit the next evening. She poured out her guilt, bitter regrets, and her despairing efforts to find God's forgiveness. When the unexpected evening of emotion and tears was over, the pastor made the sign of the cross on her forehead. After many conversations and weeks of prayer and study, she was confirmed in the Lutheran church and became an active leader in the congregation. For her, San Fernando was no longer the valley of strangers.

A spirit of oneness and comradeship developed out of a pastors' study group that met each Tuesday morning to discuss the lessons for the following Sunday. Occasionally the group listened to guests or discussed new books considered especially relevant. An intensive reading program for laymen and clergy was sparked by the director and spurred by book tables at every project gathering.

Ecumenical Involvement. One of the "lifts" the project received periodically came from the visits of ecumenical guests, whom Cliff Weihe had known through the years. The list included Hans-Ruedi Weber of Bossey, Switzerland; Colin W. Williams from Australia; Eberhard Mueller and Miss Marlies Cremer of Germany's Bad Boll Academy; Mark Gibbs, an author and lay leader in the Church of England; and Joachim Jeremias, one of the foremost biblical research scholars in the world.

Several vocational conferences were held on an ecumenical basis; the most ambitious one was concerned with "Living Responsibly in the Space Age." In one session twenty-nine scientists, engineers, technicians, and executives met to look together at the biblical and theological view of problems facing men in the atomic age. Planned by the scientists themselves, major addresses were given by the founder of the evangelical academy movement in Europe, a research professor at Stanford's Hoover Institute, and one of the nation's top young Lutheran theologians.

The Goals Project of the Los Angeles Planning Commission involved architects, planners, industrialists, theologians, and others. They discussed key issues facing the urban world of 1990 and summarized their findings for the department. Principally because of the San Fernando Valley Forum, the Valley project was credited with "setting the pace for the entire Los Angeles region in getting people concerned for the humanity of the years to come." [12]

In ventures like these and others, creative churchmen have found ways to minister to secular structures, by merging their expertise and their concerns for church and world.

NOTES

[1] Lynn G. Johnson, "MAP: Churchmen Chart a City's Future," *United Church Herald,* Division of Publications of the United Church Board for Homeland Ministries. September, 1967.

[2] *Ibid.*

[3] From "Metropolitan Associates of Philadelphia," a mimeographed report by Richard R. Broholm, September 23, 1968.

[4] Johnson, *op. cit.,* p. 5.

[5] From a mimeographed report prepared for the MAP board of directors, February 16, 1968.

[6] Linda Klein, "The Corporate Executive: A Ministry," *Chicago Tribune,* November 3, 1967.

[7] *Ibid.*

[8] *Ibid.*

[9] From an address by Scott I. Paradise, "The World Comes of Age," n.d.

[10] Richard E. Moore and Duane L. Day, *Urban Church Breakthrough* (New York: Harper & Row, Publishers, Inc., 1966), p. 101.

[11] Scott I. Paradise, *Detroit Industrial Mission: A Personal Narrative* (New York: Harper & Row, Publishers, Inc., 1968), pp. 136-137.

[12] John Wagner, director of Los Angeles GOALS project, quoted in the report of the San Fernando Valley Project for 1962-1966, p. 52.

Ministries of Dialogue

13

MINISTRIES OF PRESENCE
AND RECONCILIATION

Over the centuries the church has reached out a hand of hope and healing to individuals who are distressed. This concern for the last and the least is very much evident in contemporary churches. Not only are Christians concerned about how they may more effectively make their witness known in the social structures affecting thousands of people, but they are also trying a number of ways to reach the person who is left out of the usual patterns of organization and fellowship.

THE NIGHT MINISTERS

"She isn't going to commit suicide, at least not tonight!" This was the report of the night minister in San Francisco after he had visited a distraught young waitress who had just learned of her fiancé's death in Vietnam. The minister had spent hours helping her distinguish between the desire not to live and the desire not to live alone.

The lights of San Francisco sparkle across the Bay like a jeweled necklace, but those who are lonely or facing problems which they cannot solve by themselves are unaware of the city's glow. Although the word is beginning to get around after five years, most people are equally unaware of the existence of the night minister. He can't provide them with a home, a job, or instant solutions to marital problems, but his presence at the night places conveys the fact that the church cares about persons and their problems. Refusing to ask them for donations or decisions, not trying to substitute for a welfare agency, he offers Christian love and concern and some practical advice, with no strings attached.

Identified by his clerical collar, the minister who wanders in the Tenderloin area and North Beach, in the gloomy caverns of bus and train stations, in coffee houses and emergency wards, is Donald Stuart, ordained in the United Church of Christ. His unusual pastorate is supported financially by seven denominations through the Council of Churches.

He has found that for urban man the night can be a time for work or a time for play, a time to be lonely or a time to attempt escape through crime, drugs, prostitution, or even suicide. Because of the committee structure that fills the evening hours, most ministers are unavailable to the man who works the swing shift, to the person who is so overwhelmed with problems that sleep is impossible, to troubled newlyweds in a bar at midnight, or to the sobbing housewife in the hospital corridor at dawn.

The Night People. Like all ministries, this one is based on being with people who need help, whatever the time. Several practical reasons explain the need for a night ministry. Loneliness and despair seem more overwhelming at night when few sources of help are available. Most church programs have little or no active contact with those who work at night—newsmen, postal employees, bartenders, musicians, nurses, hotel clerks, policemen, and taxi drivers. People of the night are surprised to see the church on duty in unlikely places. Denominational labels don't matter—they only know they have been helped by "the church."

Such a ministry develops a continuing counseling relationship with drug addicts and alcoholics, the psychologically depressed, and others with special problems. Once he has established rapport with these habitués of the street, Don Stuart may attempt to motivate them toward change. Sometimes, the realization that at least one person cares helps them to take the first step. He says, "If I have nothing else to offer, I can always offer love." [1]

The people and problems Don Stuart encounters are more varied than those on "What's My Line." One night he found a hotel room for a teenage mother and her baby stranded at the air terminal after the Travelers Aid desk had closed. When he befriended a Canadian soldier who said he was AWOL, Don was able to persuade the Canadian consulate to send the soldier back to Canada before he became a deserter. He advised a college dropout, who was struggling not to become an alcoholic, to leave San Francisco and his drinking buddies. An elderly woman spent three days and nights at the bus station, eating only a bag of popcorn. She didn't know how to get home, so the night pastor took her back.

He often answers calls from those who threaten suicide or have already slashed their wrists. He tries to help homosexuals, parolees, or prostitutes mend their broken lives, because he is unwilling to turn his back on those who are usually "beyond the pale" of the church's domain.

Reading a magazine can change your life; at least it did in Don Stuart's experience. After growing up in Chicago, he spent his navy years based at Treasure Island in San Francisco and grew to love the Bay area. He returned to the Midwest to finish college and seminary and then spent fourteen years as a pastor, first to Kansas wheat farmers and then in a new suburban congregation in Lincoln, Nebraska. When he saw an article in the *United Church Herald* about forming a night ministry in San Francisco, he wrote about his interest in it to a friend on the national staff of the United Church of Christ. After correspondence and interviews by the San Francisco Council of Churches, he was called and began his work in November, 1964.

The Ministry of Being There. When Don was a seminary student, no one had developed the concept of a night ministry. As a pioneer, he had to work out most of the methods one step at a time. He quickly learned that being there is his most important contribution. His clerical collar makes plain the fact that he is a minister, although he wears a trenchcoat rather than a black robe and sits near a lunch counter rather than an altar. Sometimes he is given the opportunity to act as a reconciler or as an instrument of change for the person and his problems, but most of the time he is just there as a quiet symbol that the church does care for every man.

In his experience he has found that it is easier to talk seriously with people in a restaurant or a coffee house than in a bar. The room is quieter, and his clerical collar is regarded as less of a barrier.

"Don never approaches a person he does not know. Instead, he paces the streets, stands around in the places where people congregate, sits down in restaurants, and waits for those in need to speak to him." [2] An all-night restaurant, Sam's Hof Brau, is considered his "office," and he checks in there regularly. Some of those he has helped tell their friends about him. Referrals also come from telephone operators, hotel clerks, bartenders, and others who keep his phone number handy.

His ministry requires a lot of dimes to call his volunteer answering service each hour. To keep him in touch with those who need him most, two persons, who are recruited by local churches, spend all night manning the phones in a downtown church office. Convinced that the church should not be an office-hours-only organization, they are there to respond to each caller with sympathy and understanding. As Don shares people's burdens in the dark places of the night, he knows that he is supported spiritually by an active committee of sixty volunteers. When he is asked how he can bear this constant exposure to problems, Mr. Stuart replies that he does not feel that he walks the streets alone but that he is the emissary sent by churches all over San Francisco.

Although this ministry is structured for crisis, sometimes phone calls are not swift enough. Once a young mother tried to reach him on the telephone after she had taken a bottle of sleeping pills. When Mr. Stuart checked with his office forty-five minutes later, he called her immediately, but she died while he was talking to her. He rushed to her house and spent the next four hours talking to her distraught husband and the police. To prevent future tragedies he bought a Pagemaster electronic beeper that he carries in his coat pocket. Now he can telephone his office to get emergency calls as soon as the buzzer sounds.

The San Francisco night ministry has proven to be so valuable that relief ministers are employed to serve on Mr. Stuart's two nights off. One leads a mission congregation in North Beach; the other is a doctoral candidate at the Graduate Theological Union in Berkeley. Similar ministries have been established in Chicago and Detroit and by ecumenical groups in Saginaw, Michigan, and Los Angeles's Sunset Strip. They have found the night ministry a humbling, shattering, and rewarding experience.

Most of the people served are not as dramatic as those who attempt suicide. They are the lonely, the confused, the depressed, the stranded, who are usually surprised to find that the church cares about helping them, even at midnight or 3 A.M.

RESCUE, INCORPORATED

Suicide prevention is the sole purpose of Rescue, Incorporated, a remarkable program in Boston directed since 1959 by Father Kenneth Murphy, a Roman Catholic priest. The service has received nearly ten thousand phone calls in ten years. Father Murphy, who calls suicide "the desperate illness," believes that "no man really wants to die." [3]

He is aided by a staff of sixty volunteers of all faiths, several of whom were themselves prevented from committing suicide. They "talk men off bridges and high ledges, counsel housewives who are about to turn on the gas, and . . . arrange for psychiatric and hospital care for the lonely, the depressed, and the deranged." [4]

Father Murphy, who is also assistant pastor of St. Francis de Sales Church near Bunker Hill, got into the "suicide business" at breakfast on St. Patrick's Day in 1959 when the police arrived to tell him that a sailor standing on a seventh-floor ledge in Boston's North End was asking for him. He rushed to the scene and recognized someone whom he had befriended six years earlier, when the sailor was an eleven-year-old orphan. Using raw empathy, he persuaded him not to jump by convincing him that at least one person cared about him, that life was not hopeless. He used the same approach a short time later at the same building and again with a young man about to jump from a Charles River bridge. A great deal of publicity resulted, and more and more people sought his help.

Support from Cardinal Cushing. When he discovered that the only textbook he could find on suicide was written in 1870, he began talking to Boston psychiatrists about the problem and had a conference about an idea he was developing with Dr. Gregory Zilbourg, an international authority on suicide prevention and consultant to the United Nations. He also talked with the superintendent and the chief of psychiatry at Boston City Hospital. They accompanied him when he presented his proposals to Cardinal Richard Cushing, who gave his firm support.[5]

An office was opened at Boston City Hospital; Boston University's School of Social Work sent graduate students to help; and several rabbis and Protestant ministers volunteered to assist with the twenty-four-hour service. The front of the telephone book lists the emergency number of Rescue along with the police and fire department numbers. The number is also broadcast by radio stations.

While Father Murphy does not have a Pagemaster system like that used in San Francisco, it's one of the few electronic aids he does not use. Marked by a license plate that spells "RESCUE," his car contains both police and fire radios, a telephone with four channels, and a fire department phone. The red phone at the rectory is his "hot line" for emergency calls. When he goes out, he turns on an electronic device to record messages.

The Would-Be Suicides. He soon found that would-be suicides are highly ingenious in devising situations that spell acute danger and yet leave open a pathway back from the brink of death. One man in a motel took two bottles of aspirin and then called Rescue. Another man climbed a crane at a construction site at Boston University. Father Murphy climbed a 100-foot aerial ladder and talked for half an hour to persuade him to come down. He has also talked men down from bridges, smoke stacks, and the tops of gas tanks.

Not all of Rescue's attempts are successful. One day Father Murphy arrived at an apartment just as a man pulled the gun's trigger. An ill-timed intervention by an alcoholic mother caused an eight-year-old boy to jump from a window ledge.

Many people said they had looked in vain for a priest or minister who would listen to their problems calmly and sympathetically. Father Murphy wondered how many borderline cases had been pushed over the edge because clergymen turned a deaf ear to their simple pleas for help.[6]

One Foot in Each World. Because he has a full schedule as the assistant pastor at St. Francis de Sales Church, he restricts his Rescue activities to the most desperate emergencies and to administration. He spends Tuesdays and Wednesdays, his days off from the parish, working with James Quill, Rescue's volunteer executive director, and several of the sixty volunteers.

He finds that the combination of his parish duties and his work with Rescue helps him to keep a spiritual and psychological balance. Walking so often among the lonely and the depressed who feel compelled to commit suicide, he has discovered that their anxieties can be contagious without the balance of ministering to a parish where life is more normal and where it is usually easier to stay attuned to God.

Don Stuart and Father Murphy agree that if the church is to earn the right to be heard, it must lose itself in the needs of others.

HELP IS AS CLOSE AS THE TELEPHONE

Groups of churches in several cities around the world have banded together to organize telephone ministries. The pioneering program was started by Methodist evangelist Alan Walker in Sydney, Australia, in 1963. There Life Line Centre received fifteen thousand calls in its first year and is considered so vital that its phone number is listed with police and fire department numbers in the telephone directory.

Dialing the Life Line brings help of almost any kind from 250 Protestant laymen who share round-the-clock duty. For desperate cases they dispatch trouble teams in radio cars. They have access to specialized help through a varied assortment of professionals, including lawyers, psychologists, and home economists. The idea spread quickly to Brisbane, Adelaide, Los Angeles, and other cities.

Dr. Walker feels the omnipresent telephone is the best way to "put a mantle of Christianity" over the lonely people in a modern city. He observes that their problems "cover the whole gamut of human need, from plain loneliness to suicidal despair." [7]

A telephone referral service in Cambridge, Massachusetts, puts a greater accent on solving such practical problems as where to find available housing or reliable baby-sitters, practical nurses, or carpenters. Operated eight hours a day by the women's association of First Presbyterian Church, the service seeks to match needs with answers. The women keep a card file detailing resources in numerous categories.

Housing and employment needs are the most frequent, with many problems referred from other churches and various social service agencies. Volunteers are chosen who have tact, good judgment, and the time to give four hours every other week. Each one attends special training sessions before she begins answering calls. During the first year the volunteers provided specific help for seventy-five callers a month, for a dollar outlay that was little more than the monthly telephone bill.

FISH is a similar kind of organization which began at the Anglican Church of St. Andrew's in Oxford, England, in 1961 and has spread to many American communities. Some groups relate the name to one of the earliest symbols for Jesus while others consider it as the initials for Friend in Service Here. It expresses love for one's neighbor in such useful ways as providing hot meals for the elderly, free transportation to the hospital, or reading for the blind. No charge is made for any help given nor is anyone expected to listen to lectures on the value of religious faith.

In West Springfield, Massachusetts, an Episcopalian woman who has a maid to do her own housecleaning volunteered to help a woman just out of the hospital by scrubbing floors and washing windows. Another FISH volunteer helped a tearful teenager explain a poor report card to his father.

Usually avoiding personal publicity, volunteers have found their tasks for FISH give them a new dimension of what Christianity means.

APARTMENT HOUSE MINISTRIES

A major factor in the changing city skyline is the increased number of high-rise apartment buildings. According to *Fortune* magazine, the primary growth in home building has been in apartment house construction. Many cities are discovering that they are coming alive because of the infusion of new people who are moving to the vertical villages of midtown. Although rents are usually high, apartment living offers "instant city," with shopping, offices, restaurants, and cultural life as close as a five-minute walk.[8] Some people save two hours a day in commuting time, the equivalent of thirteen workweeks a year.

Apartments are designed to serve the "empty nest" phases of human life. Two-thirds of the residents are single, and most of the married couples are either childless or their children have grown up and are married. The kinds of people attracted by apartment living are mostly those with whom the church has never had very much in common—the poor, the single young adults, the widowed or divorced, the childless couple. Of course there are some active churchgoers who have moved to apartments when they retired.

Types of Ministry and Program. Hallmarks of the apartment house ministry include outreach on an interfaith basis and a focus on the dialogue aspect of the church's ministry. Because many people find an acceptance in small groups, wherever they are held, such groups have become a cornerstone for apartment house ministry. Counseling is also carried on, but an apartment living room is viewed by many as a peculiar place for a counseling interview.

At Kips Bay Plaza in New York City, David Rich found that the bulletin board outside the laundry room was a good link with the apartment residents. He used it to announce the formation of a playreading discussion group. Ten people signed up, and later twelve more took part in an eight-week study program outlined by the Foreign Policy Association. The following year there was a spring discussion on existential psychology and a fall forum centered on Harvey Cox's *Secular City.* Madison Avenue Baptist Church regarded this approach not as a ministry of recruitment but as a ministry of reconciliation. The discussion groups were meaningful for the participants, yet because the expectations had been what they were, no one was very surprised when only one person joined the church because of the Kips Bay ministry.

One of the nation's most unusual apartment developments, the corncob-shaped Marina Towers on the Chicago River, was served for two years by Roy Blumhorst, who found his chaplaincy to be a valuable listening post for the Missouri Synod of the Lutheran Church. Discussion groups there began with painting and moved on to modern poetry, the Christian style of life, Bible study, and existentialism, which provoked the most serious discussion. Mr. Blumhorst saw his role as coach and resource person. "Seldom did I actually lead a group, and in no case was I the heart of it. I found myself freer and more effective when I operated from the edge rather than the center." [9] He also concluded that the original nuclear group of Lutherans stayed at the planning committee level, outside of what was happening. They did not really become leaven at Marina City. Like most Christians, they had been trained in the *methods* of evangelism, not the *content,* and became tongue-tied when they were pressed to explain what they believed and why they believed it.

In the North Beach section of San Francisco, Charles Lewis conducts a combination apartment house ministry and mission church under the auspices of the Lutheran Church in America. His parish is enormously varied, ranging from career foreign service officers to members of the longshoremen's union, from "topless" waitresses at Fisherman's Wharf to the reserved residents of Chinatown, from students and artists to alcoholics and homosexuals. Housing in the area ranges from the plush new high-rises overlooking San Francisco Bay to a government-financed housing project, but with virtually no middle-income homes. Because of the needs of residents, he spends more time with the have-nots than with the haves.

As the minister of a mission church, Mr. Lewis conducts Sunday morning services for twenty-five persons in the basement of

Intersection, a San Francisco coffee house and arts center; leads a summer vacation church school and day camp for neighborhood children; and plans a weekly program for senior citizens. This is the only Protestant church in the area not geared entirely to the Chinese. He also directs a film festival and serves one night a week as San Francisco's night minister.

Shedding his clerical collar, Chuck Lewis ministers to young adults around the swimming pool of his apartment house, leads a series of sensitivity training sessions at the health club, and turns up at the champagne parties and beer blasts planned "for singles only" at the North Point apartment house where he lives. He said in an interview that he feels this ministry is valid, although he recognizes it will never reach large numbers of people. He added, "Most people meet each other through mutual friends, work contacts, or at Lake Tahoe or the country club; but apartment houses for singles are becoming a way of life, especially in California."

New Style of Life. For apartment-dwellers, the new style of life has moved from the struggle for survival to the struggle for meaning in life. In his book *Faithful Rebels,* Roy Blumhorst indicated that the old-style religion no longer fits the new style of life. Cliff-dwellers are seeking the promise of adventure, with new options and new freedoms. Often regarding their apartments as retreats from the busy aspects of their lives, they want independence and privacy. They are also apt to be lonely but insist on the right to make their own choices about which programs and groups appeal to them and which do not. Residents include many who wish for a new excitement in life, some who are joiners, and a few catalysts who draw others into their plans. Approaches to such people must take these preferences into consideration.

The Religious Outlook. A survey by Religious News Service in Washington, D.C., in 1965 indicated that over half of all newcomers to the city moved into apartments. Of this group, less than 5 percent established connections with a local church.[10] For the high-rise dwellers, God is not dead. He is unemployed and doesn't fit into their lives.[11]

Much ado has been made about the minister's difficulty in getting past the locked front door and the doorman to reach the apartment resident. An ingenious combination of research, a spy-system of other residents, direct mail, and phone calls can be used to get the minister to the resident—once. But what then? What can he possibly offer to a person who has already decided he wants nothing to do with churches or church-sponsored programs?

The apartment resident who answers his doorbell to greet a minister or lay visitor expects that a conquest is about to be made, and immediately he becomes defensive. Some residents are disenchanted church alumni who have firmly resolved never again to become involved in church organizations. With nonchurchgoers, even simple communication is difficult. The minister speaks of community or values from his background, and the listener hears from a different background. The language gap is almost total.

Because of his need for privacy, his mobility, his rootlessness, his distrust of institutional busywork, the apartment dweller often does not find the traditional program of the church very meaningful. Far too many churches are still geared to the concepts of crisis religion and family-centered problems which simply do not fit the life-style of the single apartment-dweller. Too often he hears the churches debating the existence of God or the relationship of good and evil. These are not his questions! Instead, he is asking how he can live with himself and how he can enjoy life more fully.

If the resident is at all open to the idea of discussion groups on the arts, current issues, or the meaning of life, it is likely that his previous experience has made him suspicious of the degree of openness and honesty with which the church or its representatives will approach these questions. Urban man often believes that the church is convinced that it has all the answers and the only question remaining is about the packaging and timing of handing out the answers.

Outlook for the Future. Although several major denominations began experimenting with apartment house ministries shortly after 1960, within five years most of them had concluded that Phase One was over. They had difficulty in justifying a full-time ministry which reached only twenty-five to fifty persons and promised little hope that more people would come. Nearly all attempts failed to relate small group participants to existing local congregations. Responsibility for this failure was mutual. Cliffdwellers usually preferred to wait two to five years before making such a permanent decision as the establishment of church membership. Some local congregations either did not welcome apartment house residents when they did come or had no significant programming to offer them beyond the Sunday morning service.

After a year-long survey of apartment house ministries for the Presbyterians, researcher Grace Ann Goodman concluded in an article for *Christian Century:*

> Community is personal, not geographic. . . . For people of an economic level that allows them to choose where they will live and to move when they like, housing is an accessory to, not a framework for, their life-style. . . . Housing, like clothing, is selected for price and fit and for the impression it is expected to give. No more than wearing Brooks Brothers suits or driving foreign cars is housing the basis for a community.[12]

The major exception to these conclusions seems to be ministries in poverty areas. These can be conducted successfully within an apartment house setting—not because of the shape of the building but because ghetto residents lack mobility. They cannot escape being shaped by their environment, and they share common problems with their neighbors. Dennis Westbrooks has been helping to pick up the pieces in the black community of Newark, which was torn by riots in 1966 that produced ten million dollars' damage. Centering his attention on Scudder Homes, a 1600-unit low-income housing project, he is involved with a tenants' council, community social agencies, a study center and tutoring program, an inner-city library, and English classes. This new kind of ministry also has an unprogrammed list of concerns that includes narcotics addiction, alcoholism, illiteracy, economic deterioration, and student unrest.

As for middle-income and luxury apartment complexes, several denominations are now experimenting with solutions other than a full-time resident minister. Some churches with multiple-staffs are supplementing the housing income of one minister so that he can live in a selected apartment house complex. One of the things he does as part of his ministry is to organize a program of small group discussions, which seems to be the aspect of an apartment house ministry that residents respond to most.

Councils of churches can be helpful in arranging for a retired layman to do a religious census approach within an apartment building, preferably one where he lives himself. He can probably get the landlord's approval to call on everyone first and then on newcomers, referring prospects to local congregations for follow-up.[13]

Roy Blumhorst of Marina Towers concluded that a library may be more suitable than a chapel for apartment house ministries.

Such a setting demonstrates openness, neutrality, freedom, and re-flection. It can also be used for exhibits of art and photography, as a meeting place for small groups, and for counseling.[14]

If the philosophy of the Church of the Saviour were to prevail, the church would move in every time a Christian signs a lease! At the very least, churches should find ways to adapt their program to provide the kinds of ministries desired by those in the freedom stages of life.

NOTES

[1] Stanley Matthews, *The Night Pastors* (New York: Hawthorn Books, Inc., 1967), p. 82.

[2] *Ibid.*, p. 84.

[3] *Ibid.*, p. 191.

[4] *Ibid.*

[5] *Ibid.*, p. 199.

[6] *Ibid.*, p. 204.

[7] *Time*, January 24, 1964, p. 34.

[8] Daniel Seligman, "The Move to Apartments," *Fortune*, April, 1963, pp. 99-101, 221-226.

[9] Roy Blumhorst, *Faithful Rebels* (St. Louis: Concordia Publishing House, 1967), p. 88.

[10] *Ibid.*, p. 15.

[11] *Ibid.*, p. 42.

[12] Grace Ann Goodman, "End of the 'Apartment House Ministry,'" *Christian Century*, May 10, 1967, pp. 616-617. Copyright 1967 Christian Century Foundation. Reprinted by permission.

[13] Richard E. Moore and Duane L. Day, *Urban Church Breakthrough*, p. 56.

[14] Blumhorst, *op. cit.*, pp. 93-95.

14

COFFEE HOUSE AND YOUTH MINISTRIES

Malcolm Boyd has written, "It [the coffee house] will either be playing church by candlelight—and talking to itself, amid clever new surroundings—or else be involved in real concerns outside its parochial contexts." [1] One summer in Atlantic City a group of college students expressed their concern by founding The Gallows, a coffee house where recreation and discussion could take place across racial lines.

The coffee house reaches the teenager, the student, the young adult, and the artist who do not fit easily into the family-centered patterns on which conventional church programming is based. Dialogue with the arts is a major emphasis.

How does a coffee house begin? Dr. Roger Fredrikson of First Baptist Church in Sioux Falls, South Dakota, explained:

> Whenever we have come to a church meeting with an open agenda, with great questions that demanded honest answers, with a longing to do God's bidding, not knowing the end of it, then we have known an honesty and a fresh excitement which began to free us. . . . In this spirit of openness, eleven of us gathered last December in 14 degree-below-zero weather in an evacuated fire station wondering if we could possess it as a coffee house for our community, so full of students and sophisticated younger couples. [2]

Thus the Firehouse was born. The back page of the menu says:

> It is our hope that this will be a place of acceptance, honesty, and love. Here we will drink coffee and converse and listen—but we can also ask our questions, express our hostilities, and even share our deepest need. None of us will be rejected if this is truly an open place of love. [3]

This active, personal ministry by lay persons is directed to the needs of their neighbors. "In the midst of the joy and gaiety [at the Firehouse, many] have discovered the presence of our Lord and people have been ministered to—the boy on his way to Vietnam, the lonely hotel maid . . . with no money for coffee, the angry man whose wife had left him, and all kinds of students. All kinds of people are still lined up at the door night after night." [4]

THE COFFEE HOUSE RATIONALE

The church-sponsored coffee house is more interested in swingers than saints. Recognizing that the reach of the church should be outward, those who sponsor coffee houses are making an honest attempt to meet the community on neutral territory. The coffee house ministry is one result of the radical rethinking about the nature and mission of the church which has been carried on in recent years.

Most of all, the coffee house is an opportunity to *experience* dialogue, not just to study its values. Dialogue in the coffee house can readily serve as a testing ground for the church's conversations with the world. Nearly one third of those who come to a coffee house have no sympathy or respect for the church, but they may give a more accurate picture than that given by the in-group of the church of whether the world is really hearing anything the church is trying to say.

At The Firehouse in Sioux Falls, The Salt Cellar in Detroit, Poet's Church in Cambridge, The Dungeon in Westfield, and at a thousand other locations, many people arrive with built-in hostilities to the church. If all goes well, a creative encounter between the committed and the outsider may result—an experience that is enriching both to the church member doing the listening and to the outsider doing the talking.

Confrontations with the inner self and the ideas of another help a person to develop a sense of openness and the freedom to be one's self. In a fellowship deeper than that typified by the glad hand, honest searching can take place.

One of Philip E. Jacob's conclusions in his study *Changing Values in College* was that teachers who have firmly held and openly expressed values, and who have shared them in unhurried and informal conversation outside of class, have the greatest impact on student values.[5] In this sense, a campus coffee house could conceivably have a greater effect on the values of the students than the rest of the university does.

Loneliness is a central factor in the lives of many of the younger generation. The coffee house takes seriously the homesick secretary from out of town or the boy with a beard and a cause.

An Atmosphere of Acceptance. Coffee houses are named with vigor and humor. A kind of shorthand statement of purpose can be found in such names as The Potter's House, The Vine and The Branch, Encounter, Intersection, The Jawbone, The Exit, and The Quiet Place.

Some coffee houses involve an investment of several thousand dollars, and others begin with a hot plate and a jar of instant coffee. Usually near college campuses, they are found in former storefronts, in a student center, or in a church basement. Although a neutral location is symbolically better for genuine dialogue with the world, space in the church building is sometimes the only answer to a stringent budget. If the coffee house is in a church, a side entrance helps to reduce psychological barriers for outsiders who might hesitate to enter a church building.

Settings combine ingenuity and practicality. The paintings or posters on the walls can be extremely eloquent, but few of them may be very pretty. The lighting resembles the soft glow of the living room more than the blackout of the nightclub. Doughnuts don't guarantee dialogue, but they do encourage it. Most menus feature a wide variety of coffees and soft drinks and a limited assortment of sandwiches and desserts. Prices are reasonable. To stay in business, coffee house directors must be familiar with city ordinances and licensing requirements, including those of the fire department and the board of health.

"A Christian coffee house is different from a commercial venture because it involves a committed group of people who, beyond manning the coffee pots, are trained to initiate discussions, draw people out of their self-conscious in-dwelling, and express their own faith in the conversations which ensue." [6] Their serving is undergirded with weekly times of worship, Bible study, and discussion. The commitment of these waiter-participants spells the difference between what happens in the atmosphere of a coffee house and what happens at a church supper or in a bar across the street.

The coffee house is a place for Christians to shout the gospel with their lives more readily than with words. Just as psychiatrists know that they cannot undo twenty years of twisted thinking in twenty minutes, coffee house workers know that it takes many hours to establish the kind of rapport where theology (twisted or otherwise) can be discussed meaningfully. At the same time, whenever the customers raise the question, there should be a willingness to talk about the ultimate concerns of human beings, including religious faith.

Encounter with the Arts. New art forms help to express old truths, so many coffee houses become the first showcase for young artists. Paintings on exhibition are changed frequently, young poets and dramatists are invited to give readings, and many folk singers first perform on the obscure stage of a coffee house. Performances may not have professional polish, but there is nothing phony about them.

In an extensive study made during his student years at Yale Divinity School, John D. Perry, Jr., found that one half of the organized coffee house programming featured folk singing; one fourth was devoted to poetry reading; and one fourth involved lectures, discussions, films, and plays.[7] Usually, patrons of a particular coffee house know that Friday night features folk singing, Saturday will have jazz, Sunday classical music, Monday poetry, and Tuesday a discussion forum.

On nights when no program is planned, the evening simply offers time for quiet talking and sharing of concerns. Many students and young adults consider the coffee house a significant place for dating—either to bring dates or to find them. It is one of the few places in most cities where two people can spend an hour or two over a cup of coffee, talking in privacy and yet avoiding the high costs of expensive dinners or nightclubs, or the possible risks of the parked car or the apartment living room.

The coffee house is more concerned about raising hard questions than about giving pat answers. No time limits are set for discussions; no subjects are banned. Malcolm Boyd pioneered with what he called "Expresso Nights," where each person present was urged to contribute his own deep thoughts about a given subject. As starters for discussions, a provocative film or television series may be used. Books, plays, or lectures also serve as the springboard for discussion.

THE DOOR IN CHICAGO

Surprisingly, The Door had its beginnings at St. Giles's Cathedral in Edinburgh. Even though Presbyterians in Scotland are hardly known for their innovations, they agreed to go along with the pioneering ideas of Bill Southwick, an American theological student at the University of Edinburgh. The Coal Pit opened at St. Giles's in January, 1962, and promptly became the center of controversy when the speakers included an agnostic, a doctor who discussed the implications of birth control for unmarried young adults, and the United States consul, who sought to explain American policy toward Communist China and nuclear disarmament.[8] Nevertheless, Bill Southwick succeeded in proving that the church was willing to deal with issues. Such openness is essential in the coffee house ministry.

After he completed his final year at McCormick Theological Seminary, he was named director of The Door in Chicago, which opened on November 19, 1963, as one of the nation's first church-sponsored coffee houses. The theme of its name is carried out by using a door as a dramatic sign board and other doors as a backdrop for the stage.

Open seven nights a week, The Door ministers to two hundred young adults and a sprinkling of the middle-aged, including a Spinoza-reading cab driver. It also operates a bookstore. Mr. Southwick spends many daytime hours counseling people whom he meets at The Door. He firmly believes that the coffee house must be a theological enterprise, not merely a social service or psychiatric counseling center.

THE SALT CELLAR IN DETROIT

When The Salt Cellar opened at Northland Shopping Center in Detroit, it was envisioned as an egghead-type place where clergymen and other adults might swap ideas, problems, and solutions with suburban sophisticates. But the five thousand teenagers who go to Northland on a normal Saturday discovered the place and promptly made it their own.

Pop art decorates the walls, and the teens come to hear discussion-starting talks and films. One problem teenager who had been skipping school and engaging in vandalism found some different ideas at The Salt Cellar. He still wears his hair long, but he's been earning A's and B's in school and working part time for the sanitation department in one of Detroit's toughest slums. He's thinking of moving into the community and trying to help solve its problems from the inside.

THE DUNGEON IN WESTFIELD

An informal survey of community needs which was made by the First Baptist Church of Westfield, New Jersey, indicated that a sizable group of junior high youngsters had been branded as troublemakers. Because of the reputations of the group, school authorities insisted that the young people leave the building when the last bell rang; the police chased them off the street corners; and merchants who had experienced pilfering didn't want them wandering inside their stores.

Since everyone else ignored them, First Baptist decided to try a frankly experimental ministry. An unused area with a separate entrance near the furnace room was offered as a clubhouse. Named "The Dungeon," it had already been painted in coffee house decor by the senior highs of First Baptist, but the name and the decor are the only similarities to most coffee houses. It doesn't even serve coffee!

A mailing list of eighty junior highs was developed, and nearly half of them respond regularly. They are invited to the Friday night youth dances at First Baptist—and they know that if they get too far out of line, they will be asked to leave. They also come between three and five on Monday and Thursday afternoons. In The Dungeon itself, which is "their own turf," they can smoke or play cards. Occasionally there is even some necking. In the rest of the church basement, small groups talk and drink cokes or play table tennis and other table games. Since they find it hard to communicate with their parents or teachers, several have started cornering the ministers, William Cober and Robert Thatcher, at odd hours to talk about their problems because they feel they can trust these adults.

Youthful energies have caused some expected damage to church property, such as broken chairs and light fixtures, chipped plaster, and some inscriptions on restroom walls that are hardly quotations from the New Testament. The trustees understand the importance of this ministry to the community and quietly pay the repair bills.

When any of these youngsters lands in trouble, the authorities call First Baptist Church first to see what the staff there knows about the teenager. Phone calls come from the police station, from the principal's office, or from the school psychologist or sociologist.

One of the Dungeon boys was accidentally strangled in his kitchen and died after spending a week in a coma in the hospital's intensive care unit. Several mothers called the church and asked the ministers to take over the task of telling their teenagers that Mike had died. Although the Dungeon members are usually only concerned about themselves, a group of boys turned up the next afternoon and suggested sponsoring a benefit dance to help Mike's family pay the hospital bills. When the idea was approved, they went to the best rock band in town and persuaded the group to donate its services. For teenagers like these, the steps of concern and responsibility come as slowly as man's first steps on the moon.

THE CATACOMBS CLUB IN VENTURA

A highly creative way to relate words, music, and Christian ideas has been discovered by two dozen teenagers in the Catacombs Club at Bethel Baptist Church in Ventura, California. What started as one performance in their own church has grown into a touring musical for churches of many denominations. It was also given at the Southern California Baptist Youth Conference. Recently their talents were rewarded with a weekly television series which they compose and present themselves.

What lay behind this youth venture? The minister at Bethel is Robert Rathbun, a 1963 graduate of Eastern Baptist Seminary. Soon after he came to California, he became involved in counseling and discussions with troubled teenagers. They included former drug addicts, would-be suicides, and some with police records. His own teen years were close enough so that he could remember vividly the ministers and teachers who had helped him—and some who had not.

He began with art classes and a youth choir which wrote its own music and sang to guitar accompaniment. Young people near the church responded first. As word spread about what was happening, teens came from the wealthy sections of Ventura. Now some members drive twenty miles for meetings and rehearsals.

The group is like a close family, with an age spread from ten to twenty years. The focus on personal growth helps teenagers to be honest about who they are and learn to accept themselves and others. Many teens respond eagerly to a group that offers honesty and closeness, but others find this intimacy is more than they can handle emotionally.

In the lives of some, a faith unknown before has become a vital, personal reality. The stage production of the Catacombs Club is a statement of faith by those who believe and those who are searching. "The name of the show, *Ally Ally Oxen Free,* has its roots in the child's game of hide-and-seek." Wherever they are hiding, after the first person has been caught, all the others are free and can be themselves. The members of the club agree that this is what God did for them. They can come from behind the trees and trash cans in their lives to be themselves, free in the love of God.[9]

THE POET'S CHURCH IN CAMBRIDGE

Many churchgoers take one look at the long hair, beards, and lovebeads of the "sandal people" and are immediately repelled. Those who probe beyond outward appearances usually find that these poets and artists have a valid statement to be made to an "up-tight" world.

One church that has dared to take the sandal people seriously is Old Cambridge Baptist, located a block from Harvard Square in Cambridge, Massachusetts. One of its task forces which calls itself the Poet's Church emphasizes the meaningful relationship of person to person. This group has sought to bring about reconciliation and the understanding of differences between youth and adult, black and white, Jew and Christian, artist and businessman, scientist and mystic.

The members of this mutual ministry rented an apartment on Western Avenue as headquarters during the first year of the Poet's Church. The group included Hank, a poet-genius from New York, who washed dishes and had long talks on the ego, poetry, and God. Some egos were dismantled, and some souls began to shine! Judy came from New York, too. She did all the cooking for three months, sang blue-grass songs on her banjo, and taught others how to relate to unconsciously hostile people. Then there was Sandy, born Jewish, who became a follower of Christ; also two Harvard students and a young mother.

Many evenings centered on honest, meaningful dialogue. The participants listened to angry voices and tried to speak truly. Sometimes they wrote community poems, sang folk songs, or danced to Ravi Shankar drum beats. Most of all, they tried to let persons be persons.

The first year they led an experimental worship evening at Old Cambridge, based on the Lord's Supper and spontaneous statements of the "concerns of our time." The second year they encouraged the congregation to observe the Kiddush-Communion and the Seder, which opens the observance of Passover in the Hebrew tradition. The third year they began a Discovery group at Old Cambridge.

Those in the Poet's Church feel they have a ministry to the church as well as to the world. Partially structured as a half-way house or a house church, its members are "bridge people," instruments, messengers. The poems written, the plays enacted, the experimental worship celebrated, and the dinner table conversations all have one purpose: to be the church, to be the children of God.

NOTES

[1] John D. Perry, Jr., *The Coffee House Ministry* (Richmond: John Knox Press, 1966), p. 13.

[2] From an address entitled "Journey Into Hope" by Roger L. Fredrikson at the American Baptist Convention in Pittsburgh, Pa., May 18, 1967.

[3] *Ibid.*

[4] *Ibid.*

[5] Philip E. Jacob, "Does Higher Education Influence Student Values?" *NEA Journal,* January, 1958, pp. 35-38.

[6] Richard E. Moore and Duane L. Day, *Urban Church Breakthrough.* pp. 113-114.

[7] Perry, *op. cit.,* p. 97.

[8] Stanley Matthews, *The Night Pastors,* p. 48.

[9] Frederick L. Essex, "Godly Escape," *Mission,* May, 1969, pp. 20-21.

The Unfinished Church

15

PREPARING FOR MINISTRIES
OF RENEWAL

Theological education cannot be simply a carbon copy of an experience that may have been thoroughly valid a generation or two ago. The seminary's classrooms and continuing education programs *ought* to be the most fertile seedbeds for ideas, motivation, and techniques for renewal of the church. No seminary would declare that it has all the answers, but nearly all are experiencing the winds of change. It would be easier to put a scrambled egg back in the shell than to reverse the process of seminary change!

Dr. Walter Wagoner, dean of the Boston Theological Institute, believes, ". . . few churches can rise higher than the level of the theological education behind them." [1] Dr. George Forell, head of the School of Religion at the University of Iowa, said, "The ones who succeed in the ministry are those who perceive it as their best way of serving *in* the world." [2]

These interrelated statements pose a problem for seminaries in the 1970's. About half of the entering students are interested in helping people but are not yet committed to the Christian ministry. This fact sharply affects curriculum planning and the seminary's expectations of students.

Fortunately, as students progress through seminary, comments like the following are somewhat typical.

A fourth-year student who interned in the Massachusetts State House said: "I wanted the respectability of the ministry but I was not sure I wanted the job. I still have not seen any cherubim, but I have been kicked by God and by some friends. In clinical training I found what it means to get inside and beyond myself. Now, I don't want to throw out the church, but I would like to see it changed."

A black seminarian at the same school said: "When you have

a fundamental experience of God, then and only then can you make significant changes. Otherwise, when the fires get as hot as they do in the civil rights movement, you wilt—unless there has been an empowering of God in your life."

SEMINARIES SET THE PACE FOR THE CHURCHES

Seminaries have changed drastically since they were first established by the Council of Trent. They may once have acted as a thermometer, taking the temperature of the church and reflecting what they thought the churches wanted to hear. Now they are more apt to be a thermostat, trying to set the church's temperature at the level where they feel that the church needs to function in order to fulfill its mission.

This change, however, is a long and often painful process. Even so, examples do exist where the seminaries have set the pace for the churches in certain aspects of their ministry. Sometimes the seminarians themselves transmit ideas directly from the campus to the parish. More often, the ideas don't get into practice in the church until the new seminary graduate becomes the minister or the associate. Perhaps by examining certain obvious trends in seminary life today, one can forecast the winds of change in the church life of tomorrow.

Working Ecumenicity. A curious paradox can be seen in American church life. Interest in traditional councils of churches and ministerial associations seems to be decreasing rapidly. However, newly founded ecumenical groups are springing up faster than they can print letterheads. Generally these groups are not solely Protestant, but include Catholics and Jews as active participants.

The ecumenical viewpoints of both church and seminary are as different from those of twenty-five years ago as New York City is from a walled medieval town. The "hail fellow well met" era is over. The current demand is for a working ecumenicity that pools staff, funds, and strategy planning. This approach is used with astonishing frequency in determining priorities, in staffing and funding new projects, and in acting on social issues.

A major example of working ecumenicity is the Graduate Theological Union in Berkeley, California. Both professional and doctoral courses are taught by a 100-member interfaith faculty. The student body represents a broad heritage—Baptist, Episcopal, Lutheran, Jesuit, Franciscan, and Presbyterian. Those who choose to study there need a high degree of personal and religious maturity to handle the freedom which they encounter.

The American Association of Theological Schools has called this "the most ecumenically-inclusive center for theological education in the world." [3] Bound together in a mutual destiny, the twelve theological schools in Berkeley are yet free to be themselves. "The by-laws [of the Union] speak of the importance of 'maintaining different values, of working and living together without loss of one's own identity.' . . ." [4]

One dean said: "The ecumenical experience should strengthen one's faith. You have to know what you are, what you believe, to explain it to someone else." A student agreed: "I know I'm more ecumenical than if I had simply gone to a [denominational] school . . . [and] I'll be better able to work with other ministers in the community I go to." [5]

Many Protestants in the Graduate Theological Union find they stress liturgy more because of their contacts with Catholics. Likewise, Catholics are eager to involve laymen and are more aware of the importance of preaching because of their contacts with Protestants.

President John Dillenberger states: "Education will not move beyond the impasse of the faith and order issues unless the individual students and faculty so daily live and work together that they incorporate facets of each other's life into their own beings. . . ." [6]

Those involved in the Graduate Theological Union are firmly convinced that it offers a better education for ministering to a cosmopolitan world. The joint approach is also better stewardship. Seminary presidents estimate that they can save 25-30 percent of their operating costs by sharing buildings, faculties, and libraries. Duplication of programs can be avoided. In 1969 the GTU launched a single Center for Urban-Black Studies with its staff and resources serving all the member schools.

Many seminarians are demonstrating their ecumenical convictions by planning ordination services with interdenominational or interfaith participation. They feel this is a graphic way of stating their belief that the church is one Body and serves one Lord.

Combining Theoretical and Practical. Just as the whole church has acute problems in combining faith and practice, so seminaries have problems in combining the theoretical and the practical.

Few, if any, seminaries of the 1970's try to do all of their educating within the classroom through books and lectures. Students still study the basic concepts of the Bible, church history, theology, and cultural analysis, and they do so with a greater intensity than many previous generations. But outside class activity has been added. Study in these disciplines is now focused on the growth of persons for ministry. The capacity for dialogue and ways of seeing interrelationships across disciplinary, cultural, and denominational boundaries are stressed.

Instead of just theorizing about counseling in crisis, the seminarian of today encounters crisis at the bedside of a hospital patient. He responds in the best way he knows how and then returns to a seminar group led by a counseling supervisor to discuss what he said and how he could have helped the patient more effectively. The hospital-based clinical training program begun by Andover Newton Theological School in 1931 has now spread to scores of seminaries. In addition to teaching the student the art of counseling through firsthand experience, the program also helps students increase their understanding of themselves and the whole area of interpersonal relationships.

Students learning how to preach often have the benefit of seeing themselves on closed-circuit television. In other subjects, formal classroom study is augmented by films and tape recordings, by discussions with invited guests, and by class visits to churches, coffee houses, television stations, artists' studios, ghetto neighborhoods, prisons, or perhaps even city hall. Professors have found that the closer an experience is to real life, the greater the impact it makes upon the students.

Field education assignments and internships were once regarded as primarily a means of helping students earn their way through seminary. Now many educators would agree with this statement by Dr. Paul Clasper, dean of the Berkeley campus of the American Baptist Seminary of the West: "Supervised field education and intern programs are integral, not incidental, to the process of theological maturity. Field education is kept in 'fruitful tension' with interpretation and theological reflection. Learning through doing is related to the rhythm of action and reflection." [7]

A major complication in attempts to combine the theoretical and practical fields on many campuses is a clearly discernible rift between the professors who teach the academic disciplines and those who teach in the professional fields. Part of the rift seems based on a traditional outlook passed on from faculty to faculty. Occasionally there were obvious differences of standards—all professors in the academic fields had earned doctorates, but this was not always true in the professional fields. Some students found sharp differences in course requirements.

At least two seminaries have faced this problem honestly and have come up with creative solutions. At the Covina campus of the American Baptist Seminary of the West, the faculty has developed a new teaching structure which integrates the basic curriculum content into a handful of core courses. After an introductory quarter, these core courses are taught by teams of faculty members during five quarters, with the senior year left free for electives and the development of senior projects. One goal of the curriculum is to prepare students so that the tasks of ministry will not be seen as something new and different, but as logically related to the course content.

Andover Newton Theological School, Newton Center, Massachusetts, has taken a different approach. In 1967 it founded the Department of Church and Ministry which includes three types of faculty members. The most unusual are the so-called "bridge-men." These are four professors, each with doctorates from Yale, Harvard, or Columbia, who had previously taught in the theology or church history departments. No one could question their professional standing! Three of the four professors were under forty, and all four had unusually strong rapport with both students and faculty. Now, they function as bridges linking the technical disciplines with the academic subjects.

A second section of the faculty of this department consists of teaching specialists, men with solid doctorates and long experience in teaching clinical pastoral education, speech, or religious education. The third group was selected from the area's most outstanding ministers. Since they teach part time and serve as full-time ministers, they can share with students the insights and knowledge they gained "last week," not "ten years ago when I was in the parish." These men have learned to juggle their time priorities and enjoy having one foot in each world, without being forced to choose between seminary teaching and the parish ministry.

Numerous professors have been amazed when students listened intently in their courses and promptly went out to practice what they heard. The sermon seminars initiated by Dr. Browne Barr when he was professor of preaching at Yale Divinity School are generally credited with setting off the wave of sermon discussion groups now so prevalent among the churches. His audience was widened when he gave the Lyman Beecher Lectures at Yale, later published by Abingdon Press under the title *Parish Back Talk.*

Students at Andover Newton listened to Harvey Cox and Jerry Handspicker talk about the gap between church and ghetto. Then, with borrowed chairs and hymnbooks, they founded the Blue Hill Christian Center, which now serves eight hundred people a week in Roxbury, the Harlem of Boston. Miss Judy Hjorth felt that the new concepts of weekday religious education which she learned from Dr. Wesner Fallaw were too important to remain between the covers of her notebook. She put them into practice on Tuesday and Thursday afternoons in Newton Highlands, developing a pattern which soon spread to many suburban communities in the Boston area.

Many aspects of creative worship—folk music, contemporary prayers, a less structured order of service, illustrations from secular sources, and even the use of drama, dance, and instrumentalists— have traveled a direct route from the seminary to the sanctuary.

Accent on Urbanization. The city has become the focus of seminary life, just as it has for American life as a whole. To learn more about urban life, seminaries are establishing or expanding their relationships with public and private universities, as well as other educational institutions like the Urban Training Center, which opened in Chicago in 1964 to train laymen and clergy for "a mission to metropolis." The Center seeks answers to the festering problems of the inner city: racial conflicts, unemployment, declining churches, inadequate housing, and poor schools.

To help students learn the hard facts about what it is like to be homeless, broke, and unemployed in the big city, every trainee takes "the plunge" of trying to live on two dollars a day, or he experiences a "live-in" with a Chicago family. The technique of the urban plunge is also used in training centers in Cleveland, Los Angeles, and other cities.

The Chicago center stresses actual experience, interrelationships of crucial issues, reflective thinking, and innovative planning. Since its six-man, ecumenical staff is committed to the belief that "the church is really the church when it is on mission in the world," the students get experience with a wide variety of urban agencies. One trainee may do night duty with a policeman on Chicago's South Side; another may work with a civil rights group; a third may hammer out answers to ethical questions with corporation executives; and a fourth may be involved in the city's political power structure.

Each trainee becomes acquainted with ways to deal with power structures in the church and in the city, learns to recognize priorities in his ministry, and is challenged to expand his skills for the good of his church and of the city. About three hundred students a year enroll at this Urban Training Center. Many of them are seminarians who take the one-month concentrated course. Divinity School students at the University of Chicago often participate for four months as an integral part of their education.

The broader purpose of preparing leaders to become social change agents is the goal of the Martin Luther King School of Social Change. This school is affiliated with Crozer Theological Seminary in Chester, Pennsylvania, where Dr. King earned his B.D. in 1951. In addition to a small core of resident faculty, many courses are taught by a traveling faculty of experts who fly to the campus for a week or come once a week for a semester. Every student works two days a week in some social change agency. As a King School brochure says, "These students are highly committed to make the 'stubborn ounces of their weight count' on the scales of justice, freedom, and dignity."

In recognition of the centrality and resources of urban life, whole seminaries are moving from isolated rural settings to metropolitan areas. Woodstock, a major Catholic seminary, moved from Maryland to become affiliated with Union Theological Seminary in New York City. Alma, also a Catholic seminary, moved from Los Gatos to Berkeley for fuller participation in the Graduate Theological Union. Bexley Hall, an Episcopal seminary, moved from central Ohio to Rochester, New York, to join forces with Colgate Rochester Divinity School. One transplanted professor said, "We've come from Brigadoon, from the misty vales of rural Central Ohio, to face the very core of the meaning of existence in a twentieth century city." [8]

Student Involvement. Many of the techniques that students learned on college campuses accompany them to seminary, as they seek to have a direct voice in the formulation of their education.

Seminarians frequently serve as voting members of the faculty and its committees, and even on the board of trustees. They have won the right to have more freedom of choice in selecting their courses. Faculty members cooperate in trying to structure an educational program tailored to the student's own interests. Many professors demonstrate an openness to hear student ideas, both in and out of the classroom.

Sometimes this involvement means headlines. When black students at Colgate Rochester organized an energetic effort to raise funds for a Martin Luther King Memorial Professorship of Black Studies, they received the support of white students, faculty, and trustees. Eight hundred people attended a fund-raising dinner, which featured songs by Mahalia Jackson and remarks by Dr. Ralph Abernathy and Dr. King's parents.

The next move of the black students was to demand the right to name twelve blacks as members of the Colgate Rochester board of trustees. When administrators pointed out the legal requirements of "due process" and that the stipulated times for electing trustees made the demand date set by the students legally impossible (even though the board was willing to elect twelve black trustees), the students reacted with an eighteen-day lockout of the administration building. When this neared the point of jeopardizing the graduation of all seniors (white as well as black) because of the technical lack of class hours, and in light of the sincere negotiations regarding the election of black trustees, the siege was called off. The board proceeded to elect twelve black trustees, including some nominees of the students, and the school was soon back in full session.

The Need for Specialized Education. Because preparation for specialized ministries is still largely a do-it-yourself operation, this area presents one of the greatest needs for change in seminary curriculum planning today. In 1968 a study was made by the National Council of Churches of 350 persons involved in fourteen categories of new forms of ministry. The survey indicated that 80 percent of the new forms of ministry were launched between 1964 and 1967, and 73 percent of the project directors were a new breed of younger generation churchmen, ranging in age from twenty-five to forty-five. Only 5 percent felt their seminary training was adequate.

Limited experience in specialized ministries can be gained

through careful selection of field education and internship assignments and through summer jobs, but far more needs to be done. Many associate ministers would welcome specific preparation for their tasks and a change in denominational attitudes toward them. Rather than being treated as "non-persons," they at least should be included in denominational directories and in minimum salary plans.

THE NEW BREED OF CLERGYMEN

The new breed of clergymen is idealistic and activistic. They look to the future rather than to the past. They are far more aware of issues of their time than any previous generation has been, and they are determined to do something about the problems they see.

Honesty is a paramount concern. Bringing about a confrontation may appear more important than its painful and abrasive consequences. The heroes of these young clergymen are more apt to be like Father James Groppi of Milwaukee, a Catholic priest who has taken a militant stand on housing, than like former Secretary Robert Weaver or Secretary George Romney of the President's cabinet. They insist on the freedom to express their individuality and would agree with Dr. D. T. Niles of Ceylon who said in an address, "If you want the wind on your face, you must go and stand where the wind is blowing."

This new breed was characterized by Ted Sorensen in *Saturday Review:*

> The stakes are too great to leave war to the generals, civil rights to the professionals or poverty to the social workers. . . . More and more clergymen recognize that their ministry belongs most with those who need it most—not with the white middle-class and upper-class establishments, but with Christ's favorite people, the poor. With the peacemakers. With the oppressed.[9]

Most ministers wear too many hats and have too many bosses. One seminarian expressed his frustration in saying, "You need to be a combination of St. Paul, Freud, and Batman!" Some areas are demanding less of the ministers. The church's role in healing the sick, tending the vineyards, and copying the scrolls has been replaced largely by Blue Cross, General Foods, and Xerox. But other problems related to the pressures for the minister's time and energy can not be dismissed so fliply.

The minister's special task is to help others perform their ministry. Therefore, ministers need to increase their understanding of the dynamics of power so that they can concentrate their energy on areas where something can be changed rather than on areas where the entire power structure of the church is solidly committed to maintaining the status quo. Dr. Martin Marty's advice to church editors applies to ministers as well. In an address he said: "Separate the major issues from the others. Have a few you're willing to be run out of town for, but don't split the church over whether or not the sanctuary gets painted."

Even more important is the minister's need to develop priorities and to increase the roles carried by laymen; these two concepts are directly intertwined. Responsibility for the physical plant, for instance, should be left solely to the laymen. They are probably better informed about roofs and furnaces than the minister is; and if not, the world will not stop if some bricks and mortar crumble.

Some ministers have found that they can increase their effectiveness by working more with those on the growing edge of the church—the college students, the young marrieds, the rising business executives. The educational preparation of ministers equips them especially well for a teaching ministry with such groups—if they have maintained their studies since seminary through wise reading and participation in continuing education seminars and workshops. The books in a minister's study need to be active resource materials, not three-dimensional wallpaper!

Most ministers carry a heavy counseling load. The larger share is probably the listening ministry, where the counselee wants desperately to find someone who will listen creatively to his problems and be completely trustworthy to keep his confidences. Through a brief course on the basics of counseling, many lay people could be guided by the pastor to carry on this ministry. Where the concern involves approaching surgery, marriage problems, difficulties with teenagers, or learning to cope with widowhood, a church member might have had more direct experience with that particular problem than the minister has had! Could there be a better way of practicing the priesthood of all believers?

The second type of counseling involves deeper psychological problems which need to be handled by someone with specific training in counseling. The minister could concentrate more on these persons if he had the assistance of lay members in dealing with the other counselees. He will appreciate the opportunity to refer those with the most complex problems to professional psychologists or psychiatrists.

Placement Is Crucial. In his book *Bachelor of Divinity,* Dr. Walter Wagoner points out, "The church is going to be crippled severely if the better seminarians walk out." [10] Graduates are disturbed that denominational placement systems often match mice to mountains and "lack the sanctions for matching men, ability, and need." [11] Rigorous honesty on the part of both minister and church and a regular review of their relationships are also vital to the life of both parties.

Dr. Oren Baker's study of American Baptist ministers stressed that the most crucial years of a man's ministry are those immediately following his graduation from seminary. In a report, he declared: "A man's first church makes him or breaks him." [12]

LIKE REEDS IN A RIVER

No single type of person is the "minister" type. God takes, molds, and uses all types of men in the diverse ministries of today. Paraphrasing Bonhoeffer, one might say: "To be a Christian minister does not mean to be religious in a particular way but rather to be a man, to participate in the suffering of God in the life of the world. . . . The best sign of whether a given man is a man for God is whether that man is also a man for others, a man for his neighbor."

The men and women most needed in the renewal of the church are those who know that the church can recover its vitality and who believe that "to make disciples of all nations" should not be like taking fish from the ocean and putting them in an aquarium.

A French writer has said, "The church needs ministers willing to stand for the right like reeds in a river, knowing that in time the reeds will change the river's course."

NOTES

[1] Walter D. Wagoner, *Bachelor of Divinity* (New York: Association Press, 1963), p. 70.

[2] Martha Lindberg, "Forell on the Ministry," *LCA Vocational Services News,* published by the Board of Education and Church Vocations, Lutheran Church in America.

[3] *San Francisco Chronicle,* January 24, 1969.

[4] *Informations catholiques internationales,* December 1, 1968.

[5] Marie Walling, "The Cloth Is Wearing Thin," *The Arizona Republic,* April 17, 1969.

[6] John Dillenberger, "The Graduate Theological Union: Seven Years Later," *Nexus,* vol. 12, no. 3 (Spring, 1969), p. 23.

[7] Paul D. Clasper, "The Case for Candles," *1970 Catalog, American Baptist Seminary of the West, Berkeley Campus,* p. 18.

[8] Colgate Rochester Divinity School brochure, published in 1969.

[9] Theodore C. Sorensen, "The New Breed—Tomorrow's Ministers," *United Church Herald,* July 1, 1966. Reprinted from *Saturday Review,* April 30, 1966, p. 25.

[10] Wagoner, *op. cit.,* p. 13.

[11] *Ibid.,* p. 37.

[12] Oren H. Baker, "Pilgrimage into the Soul of the Pastor," May 18, 1963. p. 3.

16

CHANGE AND RENEWAL
By Lawrence H. Janssen

For fifteen years church leaders have talked about change and renewal as though they were synonymous. The world was changing, and the church must change with it. Change was the order of the day. A new emphasis here, programs of service there, and later on experimental worship; and then small groups for depth encounter began to be reported. While many acknowledge that change has characterized the world since the beginning, the change that characterizes the last two decades has taken place at a much more rapid pace. Change is now described as revolution in contrast to evolution, but this does not mean revolution in the classical sense. It only means that old forms need radical adjustment. We have never really internalized the fact that in a revolution the ground rules are all changed. What was up is down. What was in is out. What was the order of the day has all passed away. "The old has passed away. Behold, the new has come."

What is understood least of all is that revolution is of the nature of the gospel—that the Christian is not an ordinary man evolved into a nice guy, doing good in the name of Christ, or that the church is not a group of nice people becoming interested once again in the poor and the oppressed. "If any one is in Christ, he is a new creation."

CHANGE OR RENEWAL

A proper distinction needs to be made between "change" and "renewal," for the terms are not synonymous. Change is inevitable. Renewal is not. Change can be for better or worse. Renewal implies by its very definition a movement toward an improved condition. The world has been in a state of constant change since the beginning, and so has the church. Read the history of any national board of missions, the chronicle of any local congregation, and the fact of change will be evident.

But renewal is another matter. Only occasionally does history record significant trends that can, by any stretch of the imagination, be called renewal. Change has a neutral quality. It is measurable only by comparison with what preceded it. Change merely means that a matter is different now from what it was previously. Renewal has a quality of eternity about it, for it is a state of being which calls men to the ultimate rather than to mere adjustment to passing phases in the life or history of a group.

One of the problems within the church revolving around the change-renewal confusion has been the fact that so many people have been willing to call any kind of change by the name "renewal." The judgment seemed to be that unless a church had changed something in recent years, it was bogged down in institutionalism and tradition. An accompanying feeling on the part of the renewalists was that change was good, but merely to continue in familiar forms was bad.

Hopefully, a way out of the confusion is beginning to appear. The nature of change, as over against renewal, and the processes by which both take place are being examined. It will be helpful to look first at what might be called the "change continuum" and then to turn to some attempt to define renewal in terms consistent with the Christian understanding of life and the world.

THE CHANGE CONTINUUM

Let us consider change in the traditional "left to right" continuum, with the "newness and revolution" to the left and "reaction" to the right.

Somewhere near the center is the "status quo." Here are advocates of the present system, feeling that everything about the system is good and recognizing no need for change of any kind. To the right is an imaginary line beyond which there begins to appear more and more dissatisfaction with the present system and a call to return to a former system or way of doing things. On the part of the reactionary, the call is always to "go back" to that which is believed to have had value for a former day.

In contrast, there are those dissatisfied with the present system who feel that the road is not "back," but rather that the movement must be forward toward something new. In its mildest form, renewal calls for increased effort and involvement in the kind of activity which characterizes the present. Still further to the left, the renewalist demands that the very form of the institution change in order that new content in terms of program activity might be developed. Essentially, the renewalist is saying that the system is basically all right, but it needs to be changed sufficiently to allow new forms and new ministries.

With continued movement to the left, a line is discovered beyond which the system itself is called into question, and the demand is not for a return to a former way but for an entirely new system and new activity. This portion of the continuum can be labeled "revolution." The demand is for all things to be made new.

Still further to the extreme left are those who insist that the institution and its life are all wrong; but, without a constructive program with which to replace the old, they cry merely for destruction of what exists. It is not difficult to call to mind persons and movements in the present that seem to be calling for this kind of destruction without the ghost of an idea as to what to put in the place of old institutions and forms.

Breaks in Continuity. Sometimes organizations are able to change in a more or less orderly process. If an institution as a whole is willing to take the backward turn toward a former state, reaction may be said to have taken place within the main line of the continuum. The same may be said of renewal. However, when those intent upon maintaining the status quo or moving in the opposite direction are sufficiently strong, those advocating change do not have their way and can accomplish their goal only by withdrawing or being rejected from the group of which they once were a part. In this case there is a functional disjuncture with the older institution, and for all practical purposes it can be said that a new institution comes into being.

Regardless of the nature of the break, whether to the reactionary right or to the revolutionary left, there is always pain and destruction of old relationships.

A Circular Continuum. Thus far the change continuum has been seen as a straight line. It might be helpful to see the continuum in a circular fashion, for increasingly, persons who hold views to the far right and the far left seem similar in attitude and action.

Persons at both extremes have closed minds about the future as well as about the past. They see only one way of interpreting Christian truth, namely, their way; and anyone who disagrees is wrong. This attitude of inflexibility has brought about frequent schisms within groups traditionally called "fundamentalist" and keeps them from cooperating with others on any but their own terms. During the past five to ten years it has been observed that similar attitudes characterize many who have been called "liberal." For this reason some liberals prefer to be called "new liberals" or the "new left."

In the circular continuum the left and the right meet in an area of equal inflexibility.

Liberal-conservative dichotomy. In Christian circles, "liberal" and "conservative" have long served as terms to distinguish varieties of theological views. While either term would be hard to define precisely, working definitions have been generally accepted within specific contexts. Certain myths have developed, however, and these must be dispelled if change and renewal are to be understood.

One such myth is that conservatives have a strong biblical understanding and appreciation, while liberals regard the Bible rather lightly. The truth of the matter is that many conservatives "use" the Bible by the proof-text method with rigid interpretations, essentially rejecting the totality of the biblical message.

Another myth is that social action, often equated with renewal, springs from liberal theology. The truth is that social action is basically biblical and seems to have little to do with a particular theological position.

A thoroughgoing appreciation for the Bible and an open stance toward its understanding is often found among those who hold either liberal or conservative theological views. Where the level of biblical understanding and appreciation is high, social application of the gospel is likely to be present.

TOWARD A DEFINITION OF RENEWAL

With this understanding of the situation, some kind of definition of "renewal" may now be possible.

First, let us recall that "renewal" in the past has too often been defined in terms of change. Churches which were not socially involved have become socially involved, and such a change was considered to be renewal. Our main concern with this definition is that it does not go far enough because it does not include attitudes and motivation. A person may do the right things for the wrong reason as easily as he does the wrong things for the right reason. The Christian faith is as much concerned with attitudes as with acts. Without an understanding of renewal in terms of attitudes and motivation, the Christian church will have continued difficulty. Not least among the difficulties will be the fact that many times churches change their patterns because of expediency (anything that will save the institution is countenanced); or they will be willing to endure changed activity as long as it does not change their basic style of life.

As is often the case with an emerging concept, a definition of renewal can be facilitated by a study of changing situations. Any concept of Christian renewal must include a restoration of biblical attitudes and styles within the church. Renewal, then, will be defined more by a description of a way of responding to life than by a description of a specific set of acts.

A tentative definition would seem to suggest that true renewal consists of a style of life characterized by openness, flexibility, creativity, and acceptance of the possibility of diversity. These are derived from a study of what seem to be dominant principles guiding the movement observed in the biblical message.

Specifically, several things can be said by way of amplification and addition. The church which is being renewed will be characterized by:

1. Recognition that man's understanding of the gospel is at best incomplete. Renewal requires a constant search for new insight into the meaning of the gospel for our day.

2. Recognition that God is at work through his church and in other ways to accomplish his mission. God is acting now and is not dependent upon a single instrumentality.

3. Awareness of the needs of all persons in its community, using all the resources of the church and other agencies to meet these needs.

4. Recognition of the role of the laity as those involved in primary engagement, both within the church as an institution and in the world as servants.

5. Recognition of the role of the professional minister as chiefly that of equipping the laity for primary tasks.

6. Recognition that persons are drawn to Christ for a variety of reasons and that there is legitimacy in coming to the

church to be ministered unto. Nevertheless, the goal toward which all persons in the church should be moving is to take an active role in the implementation of such ministries as are needed.

7. Acceptance of partnership with community agencies as a normal relationship in accomplishing the work to which God calls his people.

8. Commitment to cooperative church action wherever such action can result in a more effective ministry.

9. Provision for study in depth of biblical truths with application to contemporary situations.

10. Provision for regular opportunities for dialogue wherever necessary to assure that the church is in touch with the world and actively engaged in planning action which is designed to bring new ministries individually, in cooperation with other denominations, or in cooperation with other agencies.

11. Recognition that when renewal takes place in persons and institutions it affects the whole life, including worship, attitudes, spiritual maturity, and stewardship.

Whether we agree with these characteristics or not is probably not as important as our recognition that mere change does not constitute renewal and that we must engage in a strenuous effort to define renewal in ways which will demonstrate greater faithfulness to the message of the Scriptures. If the church of Jesus Christ is founded upon the activity of God in the world and if that activity is best described in the Scriptures, renewal must have a strong scriptural base.

One other characteristic of the renewed person or individual must inevitably be humility. Humility begins with a recognition that men cannot know fully the mind of God. Christian humility is a response not only to the presence of God because of his greatness, but also to our own presence and that of our fellows in recognition that we are never able to arrive at a complete understanding of truth.

For some people this attitude of humility is paralyzing. For others it is stimulating only to the point of continued study and dialogue. The implied verdict is that, since we cannot know for sure, we cannot act.

On the other hand, perhaps yet another characteristic of a person or institution in process of renewal is the recognition that the call of God is to action. If action must be taken on the basis of incomplete information and insecure premises, we must act nevertheless—with a willingness to change as soon as new light breaks. What else can "to walk by faith" mean?

If the case studies in this book are to be meaningful as resources leading to action, they must be seen not only for the action involved but also for the motivation which stimulated the action and the renewal of life which is revealed by the action.

Resources

ANNOTATED LIST
OF BOOKS AND MAGAZINES

BOOKS ON THE RENEWAL OF THE CHURCH

Baker, Wesley C., *The Split-Level Fellowship*. Philadelphia: The Westminster Press, 1965. 151 pages.

A plea that the church recognize its split-level membership in the contrasts between the small core of consciously committed people and the uninvolved majority.

Berton, Pierre, *The Comfortable Pew*. Philadelphia: J. B. Lippincott Co., 1965. 137 pages.

A blunt look at the religious establishment by an outstanding Canadian journalist, a former Anglican who is now outside the church.

Bonhoeffer, Dietrich, *Life Together*. Translated by J. W. Doberstein. New York: Harper & Row, Publishers, Inc., 1954. 121 pages.

An expression of the deep meaning of Christian community and discipline which emerged in an "underground seminary" of the Confessing Church in Germany during World War II.

Brown, Robert McAfee, *The Significance of the Church*. Philadelphia: The Westminster Press, 1956. 96 pages.

A vigorous, down-to-earth examination of the church, both past and present.

*Come, Arnold B., *Agents of Reconciliation*. Philadelphia: The Westminster Press, 1960. 178 pages.

An explanation of why and how lay people are the "agents of reconciliation" in the world today. It is simultaneously readable, penetrating, and biblically based.

Dittes, James E., *The Church in the Way*. New York: Charles Scribner's Sons, 1967. 358 pages.

The author believes that the "church is where the action is" and that such realities as indifferent members, reactionary boards, and the refusal to face the word of God may be signposts pointing to this truth.

Gibbs, Mark, and Morton, T. Ralph, *God's Frozen People: A Book for and about Christian Laymen*. Philadelphia: The Westminster Press, 1965. 192 pages.

A highly readable book for laymen sincerely concerned with the Christian faith, yet unhappy with the church around the corner.

Gustafson, James M., *Treasure in Earthen Vessels: The Church as a Human Community*. New York: Harper & Row, Publishers, Inc., 1961. 141 pages.

A bold view of the church as a human community—a center of human relief, moral concern, political order, and social action.

Hadden, Jeffrey K., *The Gathering Storm in the Churches*. Garden City: Doubleday & Company, Inc., 1969. 257 pages.

A well-documented survey on the widening gap between clergy and laymen on theology, authority, and the church's appropriate role in social action.

Herzog, Arthur, *The Church Trap*. New York: The Macmillan Company, 1968. 185 pages.

A zesty analysis by an American journalist of the sociological trap in which churches are caught when parishioners want to keep the status quo and ministers feel pressures to respond to human needs.

Hoekendijk, Johannes C., *The Church Inside Out*. Translated by Isaac C. Rottenberg. Philadelphia: The Westminster Press, 1966. 212 pages.

An outspoken Dutch churchman writes of the need for the church to go to the world rather than to draw the world to the church.

Kavanaugh, James, *A Modern Priest Looks at His Outdated Church*. New York: Trident Press, 1967.

A passionate book written by a priest about the numerous problems current in the Roman Catholic church.

Kraemer, Hendrik, *A Theology of the Laity*. Philadelphia: The Westminster Press, 1959. 192 pages.

Much Protestant thinking must be revised if one accepts the premise that the church exists to bring men and women to Christ and not primarily on behalf of itself. Laymen are seen as an integral and essential part of the church's ministry.

Long, Robert W., ed., *Renewing the Congregation*. Minneapolis: Augsburg Publishing House, 1966. 213 pages.

Following sections on the mission and ministries of the congregation, seven authors describe case histories of Lutheran congregations in mission.

*Moore, Richard E. and Day, Duane L., *Urban Church Breakthrough*. New York: Harper & Row, Publishers, Inc., 1966. 183 pages.

An unusually well-written combination of theory and examples in the renewal of the church, with an accent on specialized ministries.

Newbigin, James Edward Lesslie, *The Household of God*. New York: Friendship Press, 1954. 177 pages.

Biblical interpretations of five dimensions of the nature of the church, written by a long-time missionary in South India.

Raines, Robert A., *Reshaping the Christian Life*. New York: Harper & Row, Publishers, Inc., 1964. 174 pages.

A call for new shapes of commitment and service that will radically transform traditional Christian patterns. It contains realistic clues on ways to change the church from a respectable club to a redemptive fellowship.

*Rose, Stephen C., *The Grass Roots Church*. New York: Holt, Rinehart & Winston, Inc.; and Nashville: Abingdon Press (paperback), 1966. 174 pages.

A positive proposal for restructuring American Protestantism along cooperative lines at the local parish level.

Spike, Robert W., *In but Not of the World*. New York: Association Press, 1957. 110 pages.

Real life situations in the local church dramatize five key issues, highlighting the tensions between theology and practice.

Trueblood, Elton, *The Company of the Committed*. New York: Harper & Row, Publishers, Inc., 1961. 113 pages.

To change back-pew Christians to committed men and women, Dr. Trueblood advocates the necessity of commitment, a call to enlistment, the vocation of witness, the strategy of penetration, and the criterion of validity.

Webber, George W., *The Congregation in Mission*. Nashville: Abingdon Press, 1964. 208 pages.

From his experiences in the East Harlem Protestant Parish, Dr. Webber conceives emerging structures for the church in an urban world. These include new approaches to Bible study, worship, disciplined living, lay leadership, and the witness of the gathered congregation.

Weber, Hans-Ruedi, *Salty Christians*. New York: The Seabury Press, 1963. 64 pages.

A group study course to help those of all denominations know themselves as persons who share Christ's ministry to the world.

Whale, John S., *What Is a Living Church?* New York: Harper & Row, Publishers, Inc., 1937. 112 pages.

A British theologian's belief in a church that is worldwide, believing, worshiping, witnessing, active, and sanctified.

Williams, Colin W., *Where in the World?* New York: Privately Published, 1963. 116 pages.

The basic study book for the five-year study by the World Council of Churches on the "missionary structure of the congregation."

Williams, Colin, *The Church (New Directions in Theology Today Series*, vol. 4). Philadelphia: The Westminster Press, 1968.

The relevance of the gospel in a church that exists for the world.

Winter, Gibson, *The New Creation as Metropolis*. New York: The Macmillan Company, 1963. 152 pages.

The work of the servant church in an urban society.

Winter, Gibson, *The Suburban Captivity of the Churches*. New York: The Macmillan Company, 1962. 216 pages.

An analysis of suburbia's irrelevance to the desperate needs of the inner city, the emasculated style of suburban life, and the prospects of its renewal.

World Council of Churches, *The Church for Others*. New York: World Council of Churches, 1968. 135 pages.

The final reports of the Western European and North American working groups on the missionary structure of the congregation.

CASE STUDIES OF RENEWAL WITHIN THE LOCAL CHURCH

Allan, Tom, *The Face of My Parish.* New York: Harper & Row, Publishers, Inc., 1957. 120 pages.

St. George's Church in Glasgow, Scotland, embarks on a program of outreach and visitation evangelism in the surrounding community. It is a story of renewal, as a nucleus in the congregation begins to see the meaning of the church as mission.

Barr, Browne, *Parish Back Talk.* Nashville: Abingdon Press, 1964. 127 pages.

The Lyman Beecher lectures at Yale in 1963 concerned a pioneering program to involve a group of laymen in seminars with the minister about the Sunday sermon.

Byers, Laurence, P., *Christians in Crossfire: The Face of my Parish.* Philadelphia: The Westminster Press, 1967. 151 pages.

A motorcycle-riding minister in Berkeley, California, describes with compassion the people he meets and their reaction to such diverse issues as traditionalism, insecurity, the new morality, and social involvement.

Carter, Lawrence, *Cant You Here Me Calling?* New York: The Seabury Press, 1969. 146 pages.

An easily read book about an Episcopalian rector's struggles to revive an inner-city parish in Los Angeles. His methods include counseling, refinancing, integration, a baby clinic, weekend retreats at a Benedictine monastery, and liturgical reform.

*Clark, M. Edward; Malcolmson, William L.; and Molton, Warren L., eds., *The Church Creative.* Nashville: Abingdon Press, 1967. 208 pages.

Descriptions of efforts in renewal to expand the church's ministry, reported by spokesmen for eighteen typical Protestant congregations.

Fisher, Wallace, E., *From Tradition to Mission.* Nashville: Abingdon Press, 1965. 208 pages.

A Lutheran pastor details the transformation of a stately dowager church in Lancaster, Pennsylvania, into a congregation willing to experiment with old and new ways of proclaiming the gospel.

*Goodman, Grace Ann, *Rocking the Ark.* New York: United Presbyterian Church in the U.S.A., 1968. 214 pages.

Well-researched case studies of nine Presbyterian churches in the process of change.

Hargraves, J. Archie, *Stop Pussyfooting Through a Revolution.* New York: Stewardship Council of the United Church of Christ, 1963. 48 pages.

Some churches that did.

Holmes, William A., *Tomorrow's Church: A Cosmopolitan Community.* Nashville: Abingdon Press, 1968. 176 pages.

A Dallas church becomes a laboratory in church renewal.

*Kenrick, Bruce, *Come Out of the Wilderness: The Story of the East Harlem Protestant Parish.* New York: Harper & Row, Publishers, Inc., 1962. 220 pages.

A stirring account of the response to a group ministry that lives in and is sensitive to East Harlem, America's most crowded slum.

Marvin, Ernest, *Odds Against Evens: Young People and the Church*. Philadelphia: The Westminster Press, 1967. 124 pages.

A Presbyterian minister in Bristol, England, guides his young people in producing a contemporary Passion play on television, complete with "pop" music.

Moore, Jenny, *The People on Second Street*. New York: William Morrow & Co., Inc., 1968. 218 pages.

An eloquent journal by an Episcopalian bishop's wife of their eight years in a slum parish in Jersey City, where their parishioners were patronized and politically powerless.

*O'Connor, Elizabeth, *Call to Commitment*. New York: Harper & Row, Publishers, Inc., 1963. 205 pages.

The founding and growth of the Church of the Saviour, in Washington, D.C., which Elton Trueblood considers the "most exciting fellowship I know."

*O'Connor, Elizabeth, *Journey Inward, Journey Outward*. New York: Harper & Row, Publishers, Inc., 1968. 175 pages.

The author's simple but moving description of recent innovations at the Church of the Saviour challenges any church member to reexamine the depth of his commitment.

Raines, Robert A., *New Life in the Church*. New York: Harper & Row, Publishers, Inc., 1961. 151 pages.

Practical suggestions emerge from creative attempts to transform a Methodist church in Cleveland.

Raines, Robert A., *The Secular Congregation*. New York: Harper & Row, Publishers, Inc., 1968. 144 pages.

New programs expand the spiritual and secular life of First Methodist Church in Germantown, Pennsylvania, as its members seek to become a people of God radically open to him and to his world.

Sanderson, Ross W., *The Church Serves the Changing City*. New York: Harper & Row, Publishers, Inc., 1955. 252 pages.

Documented case studies of churches successfully adapting themselves to the changing urban scene. It emphasizes the strategic, not the sentimental aspects.

Southcott, Ernest W., *The Parish Comes Alive*. New York: Morehouse-Barlow Co., Inc., 1956. 151 pages.

The house church and other experiments used by Canon Southcott in his industrial parish in Halton, England. He sees the need to relate the life of the church to the common life of men and to express this in corporate worship and action.

*Stagg, Paul L., *The Converted Church*. Valley Forge: Judson Press, 1967. 158 pages.

A contemporary approach to evangelism which moves toward engagement in the world, with descriptions of some churches that sought such missionary obedience.

*Sullivan, Leon H., *Build Brother Build*. Philadelphia: Macrae Smith Co., 1969. 192 pages.

Verney, Stephen, *Fire in Coventry.* Westwood, N.J.: Fleming H. Revell Co., 1965. 95 pages.

An exciting story of what happened when the fires of the Holy Spirit were felt in Coventry, England, and a consecrated people emerged along with a reconsecrated cathedral.

Webber, George W., *God's Colony in Man's World.* Nashville: Abingdon Press, 1960. 155 pages.

A founder of the East Harlem Protestant Parish, Dr. Webber speaks from that experience in defining the church as a colony that exists to witness, to serve its fellowman, and to proclaim the gospel.

BOOKS ON NEW SHAPES OF MINISTRY OUTSIDE THE LOCAL CHURCH

Blumhorst, Roy, *Faithful Rebels.* St. Louis: Concordia Publishing House, 1967. 101 pages.

The values and problems of attempting a ministry in the high-rise apartment house complex of Marina City in Chicago, where residents have a new life-style.

Boyd, Malcolm, *Are You Running with Me, Jesus?* New York: Holt, Rinehart & Winston, Inc., 1965. 119 pages.

A book of contemporary, honest prayers which the author has used in visiting university campuses and such unlikely places for a priest as "the hungry i."

Frakes, Margaret, *Bridges to Understanding.* Philadelphia: Fortress Press, 1960. 134 pages.

A survey of the academy movement in Europe and North America, which seeks to help laymen bridge the gap between the church and the secular world.

Goodman, Grace Ann, *The Church and the Apartment House.* New York: United Presbyterian Church in U.S.A., 1965. 85 pages.

Ten case studies by an observer-reporter on the church's attempts to minister to apartment house residents.

Hall, Clarence W., *Adventurers for God.* New York: Harper & Row, Publishers, Inc., 1959. 265 pages.

Graphic stories of modern missionary heroism around the world, reported by a senior editor of *Reader's Digest.*

Marshall, David F., ed., *Creative Ministries.* Philadelphia: Pilgrim Press, 1968. 124 pages.

Principally reprints of articles from *United Church Herald* which show ways local churches can engage in stimulating ministries where their presence makes a difference.

*Matthews, Stanley G., *The Night Pastors.* New York: Hawthorn Books, Inc., 1967. 224 pages.

Vivid stories of ten of the nation's new breed of dedicated night pastors, who serve the lonely and the confused in coffee houses, jazz spots, gambling casinos, and bus terminals.

Miller, Keith, *The Taste of New Wine.* Waco, Tex.: Word Books, 1965. 116 pages.

A practical book by a layman of his own pilgrimage toward knowing Christ in depth and his attempts to share this discovery in small groups and in his office.

Myers, C. Kilmer, *Light the Dark Streets.* New York: The Seabury Press, Inc., 1957. 156 pages.

A sensitive story of an Episcopal priest's efforts to minister to gang youngsters of New York's Lower East Side. The author is now Bishop Myers of California.

*Paradise, Scott I., *Detroit Industrial Mission: A Personal Narrative.* New York: Harper & Row, Publishers, Inc., 1968. 158 pages.

An honest book about attempts to minister amid the stark realities of factory life.

Perry, John D., Jr., *The Coffee House Ministry.* Richmond: John Knox Press, 1967. 127 pages.

Coffee house ministries are explored in depth, from their theological basis to the mechanics of their daily operations.

Rowland, Stanley J., *Men for Others.* New York: Friendship Press, 1965. 175 pages.

The impact of ten individuals who exemplify the Christian mission in their lives.

Symanowski, Horst, *The Christian Witness in an Industrial Society.* Philadelphia: The Westminster Press, 1964.

As both pastor-theologian and laborer, the author pinpoints the tensions between the worker's outlook on life and the framework of traditional Christianity.

Thatcher, Joan, *Summoned to Serve.* Valley Forge: Judson Press, 1960. 140 pages.

Twelve profiles of men and women engaged in the church vocations.

Wallace, Helen K., *Keys in Our Hands.* Valley Forge: Judson Press, 1967. 127 pages.

Ideas and projects which are unlocking doors to a better life for the black man.

Wilkerson, David, *The Cross and the Switchblade.* Westwood, N.J.: Fleming H. Revell Co., 1963. 174 pages.

An exciting story of a country preacher's fight against teenage crime in the slums of Brooklyn.

MAGAZINES DEALING WITH CHURCH RENEWAL

Christian Century, an independent weekly published at 407 S. Dearborn St., Chicago, Ill. 60605.

Christianity and Crisis, an independent biweekly published at 537 W. 121st., New York, N.Y. 10027.

Church in Metropolis, published quarterly by the Joint Strategy and Action

Committee of six denominations at Room 552, 475 Riverside Drive, New York, N.Y. 10027.

Context, a new semimonthly newsletter edited by Martin Marty which summarizes major Protestant publications. Published at 180 N. Wabash Ave., Chicago, Ill. 60601.

Motive, a student magazine published by the United Methodist Church, P.O. Box 871, Nashville, Tenn. 37202.

Presbyterian Life, published twice a month by the United Presbyterian Church in U.S.A. at the Witherspoon Building, 130 S. Juniper St. Philadelphia, Pa. 19107.

Renewal, published monthly (except July and August) by the Church Federation of Greater Chicago at 116 South Michigan Boulevard, Chicago, Ill. 60603.

Together, a family magazine published monthly by the United Methodist Church at 201 Eighth Avenue, South, Nashville, Tenn. 37203.

United Church Herald, published monthly by the United Church of Christ at Box 7095, St. Louis, Mo., 63177.

SUGGESTED STUDY QUESTIONS
Prepared by John A. Barker

While it is good to read the accounts of what is happening in other places when the church responds to the call of Christ and the needs of the community, the real excitement begins when your local congregation responds in a similar way. The questions which follow are intended to help the church see itself in terms of its mission and to discover ways in which it can be the church for today's world and can bring men to the point of commitment where life is lived under the full lordship of Jesus Christ.

1. Being the Church in an Up-Tight World

1. How does the church show that it really cares about people? In what ways does (or can) our local congregation demonstrate a loving concern for people as persons? What is there about our church and its ministry that is unique and thus calls men to learn of Christ here?
2. What image do I have of the ministry and the role of the minister of Jesus Christ? What measures of freedom am I willing to permit the minister, and what limits do I want to impose? Do these free him or bind him?
3. Are there ways in which our present organizational structure could be changed to help us do our task more effectively? If change is required, what blocks are there to making change possible, and what can we do to avoid these?
4. How can *our* church develop listening ministries? Can we "afford" to do so alone, and what channels can we open?
5. What can renewal mean in our situation—and what will it require of us?

2. Glide Memorial United Methodist Church in San Francisco

1. Since it is obvious that change and renewal may be accompanied by tensions, what will be required of us to avoid unnecessary tension and to learn how to deal with the matter creatively?
2. To what extent does our culture shape our worship rather than permitting mission and the life of the congregation to determine this form?
3. What are the implications of the phrase "freedom to act" in the context of our church's ministry?
4. Who are the unloved and the unlovely, the neglected and the forgotten people in our community for whom we should be concerned and with whom we should be serving? What resources are needed to develop such a ministry?
5. Why is our church here? What is our "statement of purpose," and does it have meaning and validity for our mission in today's world?

3. Judson Memorial Baptist Church in Minneapolis

1. What is our honest reaction to that part of the congregation's life which we call "worship"? Does it fulfill our needs? If not, what can be done to make it a more meaningful experience?
2. What are some first steps—halting though they may be—which our church could take to explore cooperative ministries with other churches? Are there limits we would impose? Why?
3. Who are the people in our community for whom the church is either a negative word or an irrelevant force? Why do they feel this way? What can we do to change this image and understanding?
4. What is needed to transform our "membership classes" into discipleship experiences leading to continued growth in the Christian life and involvement in Christian mission?

4. Judson Memorial Church in Greenwich Village

1. What do we understand to be the meaning of the following phrases:

    "The church's role is to be a happening in the midst of the world!"

    "The world must write the agenda for the church's program."

373

How do our answers fit what our church is doing? What can we be doing?

2. If we believe that the church is still an instrument for social change and for personal and corporate renewal, can we justify the absence of the church from the political scene? What kind of meaningful involvement can it have? How does the church assume a prophetic role in today's world?

5. St. Peter's Lutheran Church in Manhattan

1. How can the church get into the world—and even have the world get into the church—without losing its sense of purpose and mission in the proclamation of the gospel?

2. If the church is to avoid a stance of isolation from the world, how does it build bridges of understanding, love, trust, and integrity to the world?

3. Are there ways in which the church can discover and meet the needs of those not normally found *in* the church building? What are the costs to be considered, and how willing are we to pay the price?

6. Second Baptist Church in Los Angeles

1. What is the nature of the church's responsibility to help its people deal with the critical issues of our day? How do we handle this responsibility?

2. What are the respective roles of the pastor and the laity in the process of initiating change and action?

3. What is the in-depth meaning of the phrase, "God is in the world as well as in the church?"

4. Are there problems of separation of church and state involved in the use of grants and federal funds for church-sponsored but community-serving programs? In view of need and crisis, how can the church collaborate with secular agencies and combine resources for service?

7. The Church of the Saviour in Washington, D.C.

1. How do we strengthen and support one another in our Christian life and mission so that we avoid dissipating strength and energy in "rescuing the *saved*"?

2. How can my church support me in bearing witness to my faith in the world—in the context of where I live and work?

3. Recognizing that small groups *(koinonia)* can come to consider themselves as the "in-people-of-God," what can we do to keep this exclusiveness from happening to us in our church?
4. What are some of the support groups (agencies with similar concerns) to whom we could turn and with whom we could serve in some of our task-force assignments?

8. First United Methodist Church in Germantown, Pa.

1. Give an in-depth response to the following questions: In what significant ways does my faith find expression in my daily life? What doctrines are really central and key to me? What do I really believe about God, Christ, man, sin, the meaning of salvation, etc.?
2. With overwhelming evidence on the need for team ministries, how can our church develop a working relationship with other churches so that we collaborate in service rather than compete for members?
3. What is the relationship between the form of worship and the function of the congregation in its mission?

9. Politics and Protest

1. Does the community see our church as a structure to be served or as a servant structure? Explain your answer. What is the church? Who are its people? What is its field?
2. How can we creatively relate the resources of our suburban churches to the needs of the city? To what degree am I willing to be involved in this linkage?
3. What kinds of opportunities are open to us to meet, understand, and learn from people of other cultures, races, and religious beliefs? How can our church become creatively involved in this process?
4. Do the program ministries of our church fit what we feel are our priorities? If not, what process do we need to initiate to match our ministries with our mission? How much are we willing to risk for Christ's sake and the kingdom's work?

10. Black Is Beautiful

1. Is there validity in having Christians employ the tactic of selective boycott, a form of economic pressure, to achieve social goals? How can we justify our answer?

2. What are the attitudes of employers in our area, including the company by which I am employed, toward the hiring of "hard-core" unemployed? Are there facilities available for the training of these persons? What are these? If there are none, what steps can we take to introduce such a program?

11. Cluster Ministries in Metropolis

1. How realistic is it to describe the shape of the emerging church as ecumenical with a developing team ministry which cuts across denominational and interfaith lines? What are some of the issues and concerns which this concept raises, and how can we deal with these?
2. What is the meaning of the word "renewal" to you? What do you feel are the evidences of the renewing of the life of a local congregation?
3. How can the pastor serve as the enabler for mission by the laity? How can he function best—as catalytic agent, resource person, trainer, theologian, or teacher?

12. Ministries to Secular Structures

1. What are some possible and significant ways in which the church (individually or corporately) can touch points of community life?
2. How can the pastor of the local congregation be helped to understand the nature and context of the problems which his people face, the tensions under which they live, and the moral and ethical problems with which they must deal in the course of daily responsibilities?
3. What is the role of the church in a secular society? Make your response as comprehensive as possible.

13. Ministries of Presence and Reconciliation

1. In what ways can our church demonstrate the reality of its concern and the depth of its willingness to be involved? What does it mean to have a ministry of listening?
2. How valid is a "ministry of presence"? What kind of person does such service require? What would it require of me?
3. What are the implications of the statement "If the church is to earn the right to be heard, it must lose itself in the needs of others"?

14. Coffee House and Youth Ministries

1. What are some of the family life-styles with which we are familiar besides that of the traditional parent-child unit? Should the church minister to these new life-styles? If so, how can the church minister to them?
2. Who are the people who will not come to our "turf"? Where can we talk with them? What do we have to say to them?

15. Preparing for Ministries of Renewal

1. Have any young people from our church entered the ministry or other related service? What are we doing—and what more can be done—to challenge youth to respond to God's call to ministry as vocation?
2. What kind of training (study courses and mission involvement) do you feel should be supplied by the seminaries to equip students for an effective ministry? What is the support role of the laity in the ministry of the local church?
3. Are there particular qualities or personal characteristics and certain areas of special interest and training for which we look in seeking pastoral leadership?

16. Change and Renewal

1. What is the nature of the change which must take place in our congregation before we can experience renewal? Who are the persons I know who are most likely to share this concern for renewal, and what are some of the first steps we can take together?
2. Where is God at work in our community? What other instrumentalities and agencies share the concerns of the church for people, and how can we support each other in our respective tasks?
3. In view of what I have seen of the ways in which "The Church Responds," how would I define renewal? What will it demand of me? Am I now at the point of commitment to the process and to the Person?